Schooling Alone

Schooling Alone

The Costs of Privatizing Public Education

Curtis J. Cardine

ROWMAN & LITTLEFIELD
Lanham • Boulder • New York • London

Published by Rowman & Littlefield
An imprint of The Rowman & Littlefield Publishing Group, Inc.
4501 Forbes Boulevard, Suite 200, Lanham, Maryland 20706
www.rowman.com

6 Tinworth Street, London SE11 5AL, United Kingdom

Copyright © 2019 by Curtis J. Cardine

All rights reserved. No part of this book may be reproduced in any form or by any electronic or mechanical means, including information storage and retrieval systems, without written permission from the publisher, except by a reviewer who may quote passages in a review.

British Library Cataloguing in Publication Information Available

Library of Congress Cataloging-in-Publication Data Available

ISBN 978-1-4758-5001-7 (cloth)
ISBN 978-1-4758-5002-4 (pbk.)
ISBN 978-1-4758-5003-1 (electronic)

Contents

Preface		ix
1	Chartering Schools	1
2	An Entitlement Mentality	7
	Students as Business Assets	9
3	Something Happened	15
	Selling the Charter School Concept	16
4	De-professionalizing American Public Education	21
	Repealing Labor Laws	22
	Take Care of Business	25
5	What about the Sermon on the Mount?	27
6	The Good Old Days	29
7	Public or Private?	33
8	A Contracted Service	41
9	"All Politics Is Local"	47
10	Deregulating a Public Good	51
11	The Myth of Self-Correcting Free Markets	53
12	Financial "Tells"	59
	Comparing Market Sectors' Debt	61

13	Espoused Theories versus Theories in Use	69
	Consumer Choice without Consumer Responsibility for That Choice	70
14	Retirement Heist	75
15	Investing in the General Welfare	79
	Privatization Creep	81
16	Market Meltdown	85
	The Issue with Long-Term Leases with a Related Party	86
17	Controlling the Nation's Educational Agenda	93
18	The Economics of School Choice	97
19	False Analogies	103
20	Capitalism and Democracy	111
	An Economic versus a Political Theory of Action	111
	Historical Context	112
	Personal Financial Responsibility Is an American Value	113
	The "Greatest Generation" Got It Right	114
	Scientific Management	117
21	A Corporate Culture	119
	A Financial House of Cards	123
	Real Estate Acquisition Companies	127
	Exacerbating the Debt Problem	128
	Long-Term Leasing Commitments with Related Parties	129
	Underwater Real Estate Holdings	131
	Overleveraged Long-Term Debt and Commitments	131
22	Is This Any Way to Run a Business?	137
	Double Standards for Fiscal Accountability	137
	There Are No Fail-Safes Built into the Model	138
	Defining Unsustainable Losses in a Growing "Free Market"	138
	Theoretical Safeguard	142
	Threatened Educational Capital Sources	143
	Backpacks Full of Debt Guaranteed by Students' Backpacks Full of Cash	144
23	Lost Political Capital	149
24	The Role of the Federal Government in Public Education	153
	Precedents for Federal Involvement in Education	155
	Origins of the Federal, State, and Local Control Debates	155

25	The Goals of an American Public Education	157
	Communities Matter	158
	Celebrate All of Our Successes	159
26	Cashing In—Greed Is "Good"	163
	The Profit Motive: A Case in Point	164
	The Theory of the Firm	167
	New Rules	170
27	An Educational Vision versus an Economic Theory of Action	175
28	Philosophical Dissonance	179
	The Fight for Equalized Opportunity Funding	179
29	Enough Already	185
Bibliography		189
Index		191
About the Author		195

Preface

> *What the best and wisest parent wants for his child, that must we want for all the children of the community. Any other ideal for our schools is narrow and unlovely, acted upon it destroys our democracy.*
>
> —John Dewey, *The School and Society*

Universal public common schools have only existed in the United States since 1919.

One hundred years into this venture of educating our future citizens in common[1] public schools, we are in the midst of a legislated experiment with an economic theory. That economic theory is driving our public policy regarding what constitutes a free and appropriate public education and how that public good is provided for in our republic.

This work looks at the effects, not the intentions, of that economic theory of action and how it has impacted how we finance and govern American public education.

Led by the efforts of the American Legislative Exchange Council (ALEC) to privatize public education, a national effort to discredit publicly owned and operated common schools governed at the local level is in full swing. A hostile corporate takeover seeks to supplant, not supplement, our nation's public schools.

A "corporatization" of public education is transforming state and local assets and municipal organizational structures under the guise of providing "consumer educational choice."

For twenty-eight years, charter schools and various permutations on vouchers (often renamed as "choice" scholarship programs)[2] have been in existence in the United States. The first charter was authorized in 1991 and opened its doors in Minneapolis[3] in 1992.

The term "charter," as it is currently used, indicates that a private business has contracted with the state through a state authorizing agency (there are single and multiple authorizers depending on the state authorizing laws). The contract's deliverable is represented by educational services provided to an individual citizen's children.

The educational funding from the state and federal governments is referred to as "backpacks full of cash." Those "backpacks" represent our children's tax-sourced funding for educational services. This tax-sourced funding is paid out directly by the state to private businesses. "Backpacks full of cash" is a term used to symbolize the transferability of each child's state and federal funding to the parent's "choice" of "public" school.

Most state definitions of charter schools refer to these private businesses as *"public schools of choice."* Thus, this newfound "freedom to choose" is the result of the state granting parents the prerogative to choose where their child attends school.

The legislative efforts that have led to this corporatizing and privatization of public education have been ongoing since the 1970s. A precursor to allowing these "personal choices" to occur is referred to as "open enrollment." Open enrollment means parents may opt to send their child to schools outside of their municipal area or to any of the public schools inside of that district. Open enrollment is the first step on the road to taking local government's prerogative regarding the type of school a community will provide out of the local school board's control.

States electing to provide "choice" will also usually pass legislation declaring their state a "right to work" state prior to enacting "school choice" legislation. Labor laws and public education legislation are linked in the nation's push to privatize public education. It is not a coincidence that child labor laws were enacted in the same year that public education became a national mandate: 1919. Context is everything if one is to understand what privatization of a public good really means.

Since 1991, state legislatures have been systematically deconstructing "local control" of public education funding and governance. A corporatization of public education and other facets of our public institutions has been occurring at an ever-increasing pace. The same ideological forces that disdained the creation of the Department of Labor in 1913 seek to disband and corporatize public education and other "government provided" services.

An economic model of public education is replacing a time-tested educational model governing public education in our democratic republic.

Parents are referred to as "consumers of educational services" in this model, consumers in a free market who have made a "choice" to enroll their children in a state-authorized educational service provider's private or charter school.

Capitalism, our economic system, has been theorized by the privatizers to be a perfect model for operating and providing for our public obligation to provide our children with an American education. This economic model versus an educational model has created the tension between the economic theory now driving public education policy and our political and educational system's goal of liberty and justice for all.

The results, not the intentions stated by the promoters of applying free-market solutions to government enterprises, are the topic of this book. We, the public, have given up political, economic, and social capital in our communities by "choosing" to school alone.

Charter Schools don't have to work this way.

The author, an early advocate for charter schools as proposed by Dr. Ray Budde in 1973, believes that charter schools have a place in public education. Conundrums for our legislative branches and the public are a consequence of the financial results seen in the data on this privatization effort. There are too many red flags in the financial and governance data that indicate that something is amiss in our efforts to privatize a public good.

The "check engine" light on our public school's dashboard is on, and we are ignoring it based on a faulty assumption that privatization and "free markets" correct themselves.

In practice, charter school entities (sites) are referred to as "public schools" because the state government subsidizes and pays for the consumer's educational "choice" with tax-sourced revenues and generous real estate acquisition bonding based on tax-free bonds. In the case of vouchers (aka opportunity scholarships), the state subsidy may fully or partially cover the cost of a private school tuition.

To be clear, this is not how a normal capitalist business venture is funded by a free market.

A variation on this privatization movement is "scholarship" programs that allow for tax *credit* donations to scholarship clearinghouses. In this "free market," those "scholarship" clearinghouses are entitled to collect a fee for their services, usually in the range of 10 to 15 percent of the amount that they collect from donors plus any fees for overhead costs and personnel the firm may charge. All of the funding for these clearinghouses comes from either tax-sourced funds or tax credits to individuals and businesses.

Private schools are just that: private. Charters are, *by their own definition*, private businesses. The charter economic model asks the public to think of charters and existing public schools as "competitors" in what privatization advocates refer to as a "free market" of public education providers. They currently include district public schools in this mix of "choices."

The educational services of the charter or private school, *not the buildings and assets*, are what is either being paid for (at charters) or subsidized (through tax credits and "scholarships" to private schools) by the state. The new real estate owners of our formerly public school properties are private corporations.

This is not how public education in a democratic republic is supposed to work.

We, the public, have allowed our republic's economic system, capitalism, to unseat our political system's goals of liberty and justice for all.

Each day we require our children to recite the Pledge of Allegiance, which states our allegiance to our flag and republic with the words, "One nation, under God, indivisible, with liberty and justice for all."[4] Schooling alone at public expense divides us from one another.

State and federal legislation[5] has taken local control of public education out of the hands of our locally elected school boards and placed it, unfettered by regulations, into the hands of nonprofit and for-profit corporations. We are rapidly become a nation where Public Education, Inc., is controlling how we provide educational opportunities in our country while gladly demanding and accepting funding from public sources.

The results after years of experimentation with an economics-based educational "choice" model are what is referred to in this work as "schooling alone."

The political, economic, and social capital of our basic level of government, our community, is being transferred to private businesses intent on capitalizing on a public good.

These are the results of schooling alone.

NOTES

1. Even in the early days of public education, Horace Mann's idea of common schools was hampered by the general public's belief that the term *common schools* was synonymous with "pauper schools," for the children of the poor. The idea of common schools was a bold step forward from the European and turn-of-the-century belief in this country that responsible parents only needed to concern themselves with the education of their own children through their families, their churches, or the voluntary efforts of like-minded citizens. Choice advocates often call their schools "Uncommon Schools," implying that the extraordinarily innovative common schools are somehow trite and commonplace. We often forget that common schools emerged at a time when the majority of the world's governments were still monarchies.

2. In Arizona, the vouchers are listed as Educational Empowerment Scholarships, which are direct payments from the state to private schools. Another program provides tax credit scholarship incentives to individuals and businesses. This cleverly disguised form of vouchers is funded by tax credits on donations funneled to various clearinghouses for different types of private placements, the most prominent of

these funds being the Arizona Christian School Tuition Organization founded by the former chair of the Arizona Senate. A definition of who is a Christian can be seen in the schools that are eligible for this fund's tax-funded scholarships. The scholarships provided this way can favor the religion that runs the school, as the program allows discrimination by religion by carefully leaving out that aspect of the antidiscrimination standards from its definition of discrimination. The clearinghouses take a fee for this service. Charter schools are not allowed to discriminate based on religion, although many are run by ministers, bishops, and other religious clergy affiliated with specific denominations.

3. See *Ripples of Innovation* at https://files.eric.ed.gov/fulltext/ED491210.pdf.

4. Ironically, the Pledge of Allegiance, devoid of the words "under God," was written in August 1892 by a socialist minister named Francis Bellamy (1855–1931). Recitation in the schools began in the twentieth century, with "under God" added in 1954. See https://www.smithsonianmag.com/history/the-man-who-wrote-the-pledge-of-allegiance-93907224/.

5. For a concise history of the founders' intent regarding public education, see: https://www.encyclopedia.com/history/united-states-and-canada/us-history/common-school-movement.

Chapter One

Chartering Schools

The educational model for "chartering" public schools was introduced into the vernacular in the 1970s. The original idea involved chartering schools *within existing school districts. The innovation came from within the educational system.*

The idea for chartering was first posited by Dr. Ray Budde, an education professor at the University of Massachusetts. While an undergraduate student at what is now the University of Massachusetts at Salem,[1] the author listened to and was influenced by Dr. Budde's lecture in Amherst, Massachusetts, in 1973.

Dr. Budde's educational model for transforming public schools relied on teacher initiative and innovation as a determinant for unmet student needs at district schools. Charters under this model would be run with local authorization, with governance remaining with the elected school board. This governance included financial control and fiscal oversight.

Dr. Budde described charters as a model *public school system* that allowed *groups of teachers* to receive charters from their *local school board*. In turn, that local school board would grant teachers the authority to manage their schools and try new educational approaches *within the existing organizational structure of their home districts* (Budde, 1988). The meetings of those boards were and are held in public sessions open to the voters.

District-based charter schools still operate using this model.

Dr. Budde's model was hijacked and morphed into a "free-market" economic model for providing "contracted educational services" with private vendors.

Credit for this new model for the delivery of public education as a contracted service with a private free market business goes to Dr. Milton Friedman, an economist from the University of Chicago, and to vigorous lobbying by prochoice advocacy groups, particularly ALEC (the American Legislative Exchange Council),[2] a group that has always sought to privatize public services.

Greater budgetary freedom (not carte blanche) was granted to the educators starting public charters in Dr. Budde's model. Curriculum and financial transactions related to these district charters were left to the teachers, who created these new independent sites or schools within a school *as long as those transactions conformed to local board policies regarding competitive bidding and the approval of expenditures.*

Dr. Budde's locally controlled model enticed educators like the author of this book into promoting a charter model that would *supplement, not supplant*, the traditional public schools within and outside of our district's boundaries. The charters our teachers proposed and created in New Hampshire followed the original charter model.

As of January 2019, there were forty-four states (including the District of Columbia) with charter school legislation on their books. What has evolved and been sold to the public as "Freedom of Choice" has all of the elements of a classic business marketing strategy known as "bait and switch."

The charter industry promised one thing and then lobbied for, legislated, and delivered another. The stated intentions of charter legislation do not match the outcomes evident in the data on charter finances, academic performance, and governance.

In the current version of "public" charter schools, the name "public charter school" was kept while the locally controlled governance model was jettisoned. An idea of the extent of private ownership of public school assets is presented in table 1.1 along with funding option data. There are forty-four states with charter legislation as of January 2019.

States with the most restrictive ownership or real estate funding options are rated low by choice advocacy raters. The model, idealized, insists on private real estate ownership and liberal tax-free bond funding for the purchase of that real estate.

Governance by a locally elected school board has been supplanted by a CEO/corporate board[3] model. The innovative educational model Dr. Budde

Table 1.1. State Funding and Tax-Free Bond Support of Charter School Properties

State Dedicated Facilities Funding	State Grant Programs	Tax-Exempt Bonds	State Credit Enhancement	For Profits Allowed	Private Owner Allowed
11 States	13 States	33 States	6 States	21 States	23 States

was advocating for was co-opted and turned into a long-range plan to replace district public schools with privately held charters and private school vouchers. An intentional hostile corporate takeover of public education has been launched.

The word *vouchers*[4] in Dr. Friedman's model, which was always greeted with skepticism by the public, has been replaced with the phrase "Educational Opportunity Scholarships." Marketing language strategies abound in the world of corporate solutions for our educational "marketplaces."

The "profit motive," considered a key component of a capitalist free-market model, was promoted by the charter industry as a way to provide "free-market incentives" that would entice entrepreneurs to invest in a newly emerging educational services marketplace. As in most "free markets," this entailed the acquisition and capitalization of real estate and business assets. Unlike true "free markets," the capital for this market is publicly sourced.

Charter economic theory predicted that a charter holder's financial success would come from an efficient delivery of improved academic performances through the application of business financial and governance models to the management of our public schools.

An exit theory that predicted parents would exit academically under-performing public and charter schools was posited. This consumer model predicted parents would "choose" based on academic performance criteria. Customer service and efficient delivery of educational services would be a hallmark of the new choice model.

Financed by public funding and run by CEOs rather than educators, the model encouraged corporate governance with oversight in the hands of an appointed corporate board. Owner-appointed "governing boards" at the local charter level would "vote" on budgets and school operations. The number of members and the composition of those boards is normally left to the charter corporate owner. Boards of one person or two married individuals are not uncommon in the data.

The once-sacrosanct theory that local control of education should rest in the hands of an elected school board was bypassed by providing direct payments for educational services by the state to educational service corporations organized as either "for profits" or 501 C 3 nonprofit entities. How those funds were then spent was up to the CEO/owners. In theory, the money, once paid to the contractors, becomes their property to spend as they see fit.

Government regulations were removed while government funding and financing was kept. Great freedom was granted without the accompanying great responsibility that the public assumes comes with any use of publicly sourced funding.

The model was sold as a fiscally "conservative" solution.

Ronald Reagan dispelled the notion of trusting promises, treaties, or contracts without verifying the results when he succinctly stated, "Trust, but verify" while dealing with the Soviet Union on nuclear arms agreements. That conservative principle has been left out of charter legislation. Verification of financial results and practices was the first thing charter legislation "deregulated."

The espoused charter economic model counts on unrestricted financial freedom for the corporate contractor once the state has paid the contracted amount agreed upon for educational services. The amounts designated for charter schools are added to state budgets proposed by and voted on by the state legislature and approved by the governor. The same governmental bodies still, rightfully, legislate how public school districts must conduct business.

Most state public education legislation still allows[5] for the local community to raise additional funding for their local public schools (i.e., budget overrides and building projects). These expenditures are placed before the voters by the local school board at public meetings or on special ballot measures. Limits on the amount of debt that a district can assume are regulated and stated in state and local laws and policies.

No such restriction applies to charter contractors in states that are termed, by industry advocacy groups, "choice-friendly" states. Charter corporate and governing boards are not elected. They are appointed by corporate owners. They "answer" to the state charter board regarding academic and financial performance.

In most states, multiple state "authorizing agencies" authenticate charter applicants as state-authorized contractors for educational services. *In the majority of states with charter legislation, there are no requirements for the corporate management team to have an educational pedigree.*[6]

There are also no specifications or rules that require a management degree or MBA for these newly minted "CEOs."

The legislation in most charter states is intentionally giving the state the prerogative to "contract out" the states' constitutional (state constitution) obligation to provide a "free and appropriate" public education to its children. This contracting scheme deliberately bypasses the local communities' publicly elected school boards' policies and procedures. This is referred to as "deregulation."

Only *thirteen of the forty-three*[7] *states with charter laws have any provisions for local school boards to oversee charter school finances.* The majority of those states also have other charter authorizers eligible to authorize and oversee charters.

Once charters are "authorized," that *authorization* allows the charter contractor to collect educational funding from the state for *contracted educa-*

tional services. The state funding amounts can also include any *extra funding* provided by the state through charter legislation. In practice, charters receive more money from *state sources* than local districts.

The charter industry is quick to point out that districts, and in some states charters, can draw additional funding from local taxes and bond issues for construction of school facilities.

Districts can also receive extra funding from their state government for capital projects, transportation, and other large-ticket items. Those state sources of funding depend on the state legislature authorizing and voting to raise those funds through taxation.

The property and assets in a district remain public, not private, property.

The federal government colludes with and subsidizes this contracting scheme by allowing federal grants for specialized educational services to be paid out to charter contractors in the same manner. These federal funds are delivered as block grants to the states. The money then follows the child to his or her parents' school of "choice."

Federal funds are supposed to supplement, not supplant, the funds that the receiving entity is receiving from the state to provide educational services. The legal basis for these contracting service transactions is codified in the limited charter school laws in each state. Those laws vary from state to state.

This reflection on the effects of privatization on our public schools looks at what the public loses politically, economically, and in social capital as a result of schooling outside of our communities' school systems.

This work is not written as an anti-charter tome. Ten years in Arizona charters as a corporate officer, charter representative, principal, and superintendent, and thirty years in New Hampshire public district schools and colleges, inform this work. It is informed by hard data gathered by a research practitioner with an insider's experience of every aspect of public and charter schools.

The results, not the intentions, of an economic model regarding the social responsibility of a business operating in an area defined as a public good are the focus of this work.

The political, economic, and social costs of "schooling alone" at the privatized schools we have "chosen" are mounting.

We have acted on the wrong set of ideals for our publicly funded schools.

The results are narrow and unlovely, and as John Dewey warned us, they are destroying our democracy. They are also bankrupting our funding for our future citizens' education.

These are the results of "schooling alone."

NOTES

1. Started in 1854 with a student body of only female students, Salem Normal School was born of the humanitarian efforts of Horace Mann. Mann, who took over John Quincy Adams's seat in Congress, went on to become a pioneer in the practice of bringing education to all children no matter their socioeconomic status. He viewed education in a republic as an equalizer.

2. See also: https://www.exposedbycmd.org/?gclid=EAIaIQobChMIy_fe-7Od4AIVDtlkCh37nAS2EAAYASAAEgLcQfD_BwE.

3. In Arizona, the model allows for a one- or two-person corporate board. The CEO is often on the board or the only member of the board. In cases where the board is composed of two people, they are usually either married or related. Most charters try to avoid this configuration; however, the "rules" allow it.

4. Vouchers have always had a difficult time when the matter has been put to a public referendum.

5. This model is under attack under the guise of what charter advocacy groups term "True Backpack Funding," a move to eliminate local communities' ability to determine their own levels of educational funding by usurping this ability and replacing it with state-level funding of public education via state taxes on property, which provides a generalized funding level. It is a march of folly designed to eliminate local fiscal control of public education funding.

6. The author worked in a charter group in which two principals had only high school diplomas on their curriculum vitae.

7. The District of Columbia's charter laws make it the forty-fourth political unit to allow charter schools within its geographical boundaries.

Chapter Two

An Entitlement Mentality

Conservative capitalistic solutions are supposed to be opposed to the idea that citizens are entitled to government-provided services.

"School choice" is theorized to give individual citizens the ability to take charge of the money, "backpacks full of cash," that the state and federal governments would have spent funding a public education for their child. They are then given the "freedom" to use those funds to pay for their personal educational "choice."

This entitlement to government funding for an individual's choice of school is euphemistically referred to as "freedom to choose" by the charter industry. This catchphrase is usually truncated to one word, *choice*. Charters and voucher advocates advertise these government-paid contracting fees as "free tuition." Free, in this case, means subsidized by the government—that is, the taxpayer.

Critics of any research that questions charter financing or governance often use the word *socialists* to describe the authors of those critiques. They paint the research as "anti-choice." The industry then cites "mom and pop" charters that are in the data. We have already noted that these exemplars exist (they make up 23 percent of all charters).

Most of the scholarship programs in the states start as small-scale efforts to provide "choice" for handicapped children, veterans, or "bullied" children. This begs the question regarding open enrollment choices, charter choices, and the parent's right to seek out specialized placements under special education laws. An emotional play is often used as the means to get the camel's nose into the tent of privatizing public education[1] even further.

In the case of "tuition scholarships," the funds are put onto voucher debit cards and are then given to the parents to use at the private school of their choice, replicating the use of debit cards in the oft-criticized USDA Food

Stamp program. Unsurprisingly the misuse and abuse rate is 10 percent with both types of vouchers.

Public outcry regarding Common Core's federal intrusion into local education does not extend to the federal government supplanting local education entirely by supporting free-market chartering "freed" from local democratically elected fiscal oversight.

Additional charter replication and expansion funding, nationally in the billions of dollars, is also available from the U.S. Department of Education. These funds can be used to either start up or expand (replicate) academically and financially successful charter schools. The most recent of these USDOE grants are titled "Charter Credit Enhancement" grants. This in spite of numerous and current USDOE audit concerns[2] regarding how those funds are accounted for.

This new round of federal grants to charter schools was designed and purposed at the behest of charter advocacy groups. Their purpose is to provide credit enhancements to either financially weak or rapidly expanding (*charter replication* is the term used) charter companies. These credit enhancements enable charter contractors to access and leverage the tax-free bonds that fund the buildings and assets held and owned by these private businesses at a lower interest rate than those assets would command in a commercial lending market.

As a result of this government largesse, and generous loan funding terms, charters have amassed a debt-to-property ratio of 1 to .55 in Arizona. Over the course of twenty-five years, a charter real estate debt bubble has been created thanks to misplaced lending incentives and unbridled charter growth.

Sudden catastrophic financial closures of charter schools *during the school year* are omens that something is amiss in the world of charter school finances. Nineteen percent of all financially caused charter closures occurred *during the academic year*.[3] This means the contracted educational service was not delivered. Another ominous sign is the number of charter holders that voluntarily give up their charter each year at the end of the year.

There is no viable correlation between a charter's academic ratings and the charter financial failure statistics. There is also no consistent correlation between charters' financial success and their academic performance in the data.

A typical business owner does not "give up" a business that is thriving. Financial distress is usually the motivation for surrendering a charter. Bankruptcies and charter firms rated as "Going Concerns" on their audit are all too common in the data. The "Going Concern" rates are increasing, not decreasing.

As the national data on charter school closures shows, most of these failures impact our most vulnerable student populations.

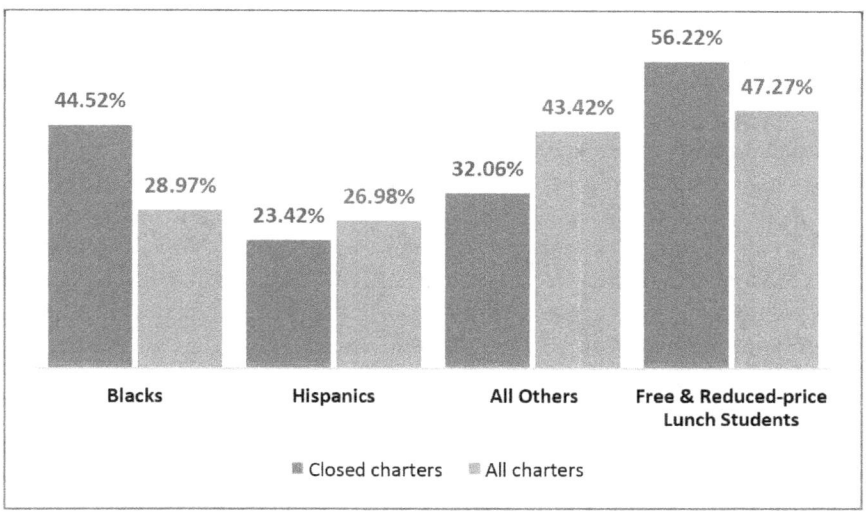

Figure 2.1. Students in Charters That Closed versus All Charters, by Ethnicity and Poverty, 2000–2015

STUDENTS AS BUSINESS ASSETS

Student average daily membership is counted as a revenue asset on charter bond issues. One of the ways these "assets" are leveraged as collateral on this mounting charter debt is by claiming the *anticipated* revenues from the charter holders' "contracted" Equalized Educational Opportunity funding, that is, the "backpacks full of cash" and any additional funding for charters provided by the state.

The revenue value represented by the students' "backpack full of cash" is used in a similar manner as a homeowner trying to claim or falsifying their anticipated income[4] to justify the mortgage loan's potential value. Unlike a mortgage loan, potential income represented by *anticipated* student counts, known as ADM (Average Daily Membership), can be counted as a revenue asset when the charter's property owner borrows tax-free bond money.

The pre-counting of anticipated revenue allows charter holders to leverage their property and assets beyond the monetary value of those physical assets. The term that most people are familiar with for properties that are overleveraged as a result of the anticipated values not coming in is *under water*. Twenty-five years of applying this real estate financing model are now available.

Arizona is a state that is highly rated by charter advocacy groups for its "choice friendliness." Charter properties in Arizona are "under water" by over $1.6 billion as of June 2018. Four years of data indicates that this real estate bubble is growing *at a faster rate than charter property values*. The financial problems are growing, not receding.

As of June 30, 2017, the charter industry *as a whole* was overleveraged and under water. Eighty-eight percent of 579 charter sites in Arizona were in this condition (under water) at the end of fiscal year 2017. The issue is reflected and manifested in sudden catastrophic closures during the school year, eighty-two in Arizona, and in the 43 percent rate of charter failures in this free-market sector since 1995. No one, except in the case of limited and documented fraudulent transactions, meant for this to happen.

The borrowing largesse subsidized by tax-free bonds is similar to the 100- to 125-percent-of-value mortgages prior to the last market crash. These terms allowed homeowners to borrow more than their incomes could easily support. The charter holder became "property poor."

Fannie Mae and Freddie Mac, quasi-governmental mortgage lenders, and the bundling of mortgage debt by Wall Street firms, along with "sunny" rating agency reports, were causes of the 2007–2008 mortgage market meltdown. It's happening again.

Lopsided real estate figures[5] *show:*

- *Arizona charter companies hold 33 percent of all school property debt.*
- *Arizona charters hold less than 7 percent of all of the school properties and assets (district and charter) in the state.*
- *Charters educated a statistically high percentage (16 percent) of all Arizona school-aged children as of fiscal year 2017. California has a higher proportion, with the average in the other charter states running at 10 percent of all students.*
- *The majority of charter bonds are either unrated or junk bond grade, an indication of the properties' risk factors.*

Other types of "choice options" are also consuming our public education funding sources.

In the case of "opportunity scholarships," state debit cards are provided to cover *educational costs* associated with a private school education. These, as noted, function like the USDA debit cards used by food stamp recipients.

One version of government debit cards, food stamps, is called "welfare." The other form is deemed to be an "empowerment scholarship." As one might suspect, there are abuses of these debit card funds in both cases, even though both ends of the socioeconomic scale are present in these two versions of debit cards. *Statistically, the abuse rates for both are remarkably similar in scope (around 10 percent).*

In several choice-friendly states, parents can also apply for tax credit-funded scholarships from private businesses set up to solicit, collect, and distribute those scholarships. Parents can tap in to multiple "scholarship" clearinghouses in order to secure several sources of scholarship funds. These funds may then be used at the parents' "choice" of private school.

This form of scholarship can be, and in 55 percent of cases is, used at religiously-oriented private schools. Ostensibly, this use of *parent-selected placements* keeps the state out of the separation of church and state issues one associates with public schools. This political stance regarding the separation of church and state is justified by noting that the parents, not the state, are paying the vendor with the scholarship money—a sleight-of-hand maneuver.

On average, these "private school scholarships" cost the state $2,700 *more* per student than the same child would cost if the parent "chose" a charter school.[6] The source of those funds, tax credits to individuals and businesses, have been transformed into "scholarship money" by the scholarship clearinghouses that are profiting from these transactions (10 to 20 percent of the gross).

Arizona, a state that is highly rated by charter advocacy groups as "choice-friendly," also provides extra funding to acquire additional properties and pay for charters' committed leases. Those long-term leases are often with related-party firms (77 percent of all cases) that hold the charter's property and assets. *Charter properties and assets are still deemed to be private property, despite the extra funding's source (taxpayer-funded resources).*

The logic behind the bigger state per-pupil payout for charters is that these private charter companies cannot seek operating or building funds through local elections the way district schools frequently do via bonds and overrides[7]; as private contractors, charter holders are free to spend this money, the additional funding, *as they see fit* to run their private business.

How is all of this possible?

The supplanting of public education with private contracting has been legitimized and legalized. State law, in most states with charter legislation, designates charter holders as the owners of all of the property and assets that they accumulate in the course of doing business inside of, or outside of, the state. The charter holder is also authorized to use that property *and the expected revenues from equalized educational funding* to take on long-term (and short-term) debt.

The caveat is that they must produce academic results.

This is all marketed as a new educational "innovation."

It isn't.

Contracted services *have always existed, when approved by the school board, at district schools.*

This bears repeating: Contracting for educational services is not a new educational innovation. In some states, like New Hampshire and Vermont, several school districts *have always contracted* with private schools for their high school programs rather than start their own public high schools. Those symbiotic relationships saved money and created efficiencies for local taxpayers and those private enterprises.

Supervisory unions, the educational management entities set up for the management of single and multiple district schools, may also elect to provide a regional high school for the area's elementary schools. This arrangement is a form of contracted educational service that already operated within the existing scope of public schools. Local control of spending remains with the school board. These types of contracting arrangements, while creating efficiencies and saving money, do not supplant the local school board's fiscal control of taxpayer-sourced funds.

Typically, public educational management entities charge between 4 and 9 percent of the gross amount of funding raised by a local district. Charter educational management firms critiqued in our reporting on related party transactions had to be charging upwards of 15 to 99 percent of a charter school's[8] revenue to be dinged for price gouging for this "service." One firm was charging 94 percent.

These public-private partnerships at districts were initiated at the local level prior to 1991, with some of these synergetic relationships dating back to the nineteenth century. When allocating state funds to those district and private partnerships, the state funding *along with local funding* "follows" the student to the private high school.

Districts also will often contract out specialized placements of special needs students. This type of specialized private placement was expanded under Federal Law 94-142 in 1975.

Voucher and "opportunity scholarships" are often justified and initiated as a means to allow parents of special needs children, children of veterans, and children who are being "bullied" to send their child to a private placement. Veterans and "bullied children" already have access to other district programs and charter schools in those states pushing for even more "choices."

A special education "choice" was already available to special needs children; however, an educational need and justification for that alternative placement needed to be established through an IEP. This process protects the people funding that placement, the taxpayers.

An Individual Educational Plan (IEP) under the provisions of the special education laws (Public Law 94-142) provides the mechanism for this placement to occur. The educational contractors providing the placement make money (profit) on this arrangement, and the district fulfills its obligation to provide a free and appropriate education to the special needs student.

The district and the parents have an equal voice in these special needs placements under the guidelines of Public Law 94-142. Since 1975, this federal law has dramatically affected the cost of a free and appropriate education as districts (local education agencies, or LEAs) became responsible for special needs students within their boundaries ranging from three to twenty-two years of age.

In contrast to these locally initiated district/private contracts, chartering and vouchering private education have been instituted from the top down. The state and federal government levels have legislated these new rules for "public" education. State legislatures have enacted legislation[9]—which in most charter states takes the community level of government out of the authorizing process—governance, and the fiscal oversight of charter firms.

Recognizing this oversight problem, several states with charter laws preserved this historic link with local government and local control. However, many of those states also allow multiple authorizers, typically universities and state charter boards. *The connection of charter schools to the community has been intentionally left in place in those states.*

In some states, charters are not allowed to own the physical property in which they operate their businesses.

In others states, charter legislation ensures that the charter holder is the sole owner of the property and assets and retains complete financial control of educational revenue payments received as a part of their contract with the state for educational services.

As a private business CEO, the charter holder retains the option of using those assets to acquire bonding and long-term debt and the right to commit the charter to long-term leases with related subsidiaries of the charter company. CEOs, corporate boards, and governing boards at the charter level have supplanted local school board governance models.

Charters *don't have to operate this way*. They choose to by choosing which economic theory's stance on the social responsibility of a business they are operating under.

Milton Friedman believed and stated that "the only social responsibility of a business is to make a profit for its shareholders." Those shareholders were then free as individuals to use their gains to promote and pay for their personal choices regarding their contributions to the social well-being of their community.

There are alternative economic theories regarding the social responsibility of businesses. One of those theories states that businesses should balance profit-making activities with activities that benefit society. "It involves developing businesses with a positive relationship to the society in which they operate. The International Organization for Standardization (ISO) emphasizes that a business's relationship to its society and environment is a critical factor in operating efficiently and effectively."[10]

What has happened to running our schools for the public good?

NOTES

1. After voters overwhelmingly denied an expansion of private school scholarships, an Arizona legislator attempted to use the claim of "bullying" as a premise to reintroduce private school funding initiatives. Predictably, ALEC ran a piece in the *Arizona Republic* on the need for this program. The letter to the editor came from its national spokesman.

2. See also: https://www.washingtonpost.com/news/answer-sheet/wp/2015/11/05/the-not-to-be-believed-letter-sent-by-u-s-education-department-to-ohio/?noredirect=on&utm_term=.11cef15f64cd.

3. This work is backed up by multiple research studies located and free for download at www.grandcanyoninstitute.org. The documents contain all of the citations and direct links to the source data.

4. One of the reasons so many mortgage loans failed was that lenders were not checking on the incomes claimed by borrowers during the height of the mortgage bubble. The reason a homeowner has to show income from the prior tax year with actual W-4 and other income sources listed is to ensure that the borrower can pay their mortgage.

5. See: Red Flags: Overleveraged Properties at www.grandcanyoninstitute.org for detailed statistical analysis of this overleveraging issue.

6. See: http://grandcanyoninstitute.org/wp-content/uploads/2018/09/GCI_Policy_Private_School_Program_Costs_2018_Sept_5_2018.pdf.

7. Since the passage of charter and vouchering laws, there has been a marked decrease in the passage of these district bonds and overrides. "Why should I vote for a bond that will raise my taxes when my children go to a charter (private) school?" This statement has been heard more than one time by the author on the sidelines of a soccer field. The loss of social capital in our communities is readily apparent in this kind of my school, their school mindset.

8. See: Red Flags: Related Party Transaction at www.grandcanyoninstitute.org for a detailed analysis of this issue. Also see USDOE Final Management Information Report: Charter School Vulnerabilities *X42K0002 - Charter School Vulnerabilities (PDF) - ED.gov.*

9. Typically, the state will initiate an "open enrollment" rule prior to allowing charter contracting. This rule enables parents to send their child to another district or a different local school within the district.

10. Source: Investopedia: https://www.investopedia.com/terms/s/socialresponsibility.asp.

Chapter Three

Something Happened

Dr. Budde's original model for charters works. It is the model this author bought in to back in 1973 and engineered into his public school district in 1999. The author's New Hampshire school district received substantial funding from a Public Charter School Startup federal grant in fiscal year 2000. This was part of a federal grant to *start public, district-based charter schools* in New Hampshire (Monadnock Regional Public Schools of Choice, MRPSOC).

The schools created there still exist. These charters do cost *less to run while staying connected to the communities in which they operate*. Political, economic, and social capital grow in this version of charter schools. They supplement what is going on in the community's public schools rather than attempting to supplant it. Our data shows that approximately 23 percent of the charter operators in the United States behave in this manner. Good for them.

The problem is that 77 percent do not.

When the public reads about charter school corruption and transactions that seem to be questionable, they react with calls for charter school and voucher oversight. This intuitive revulsion is deep-seated and comes from our sense of right and wrong regarding the use of public funds. The unwritten laws according to which we operate and with which we make sense of the world have been disturbed.

We are influenced by our upbringing as citizens in a democratic republic. That upbringing is imbued with both Western and Eastern religious values. Capitalism is a great economic engine that is rightfully defended as a working model for our economy. This does not mean that it correlates perfectly with the ideals espoused by our republic's goal of "liberty and justice" for all.

The existing charter model as legislated confuses a capitalist economic model with the educational goal of providing an American education to our citizens. We have been sold a permutation of Dr. Budde's model for innovating our public schools devoid of its guiding governance and fiscal oversight model.

SELLING THE CHARTER SCHOOL CONCEPT

According to the National Conference of State Legislatures:

> Charter schools are publicly funded, privately managed and semi-autonomous schools of choice. They do not charge tuition. They must hold to the same academic accountability measures[1] as traditional schools. They receive public funding similarly to traditional schools. However, they have more freedom over their budgets, staffing, curricula and other operations. In exchange for this freedom, they must deliver academic results and there must be enough community demand for them to remain open.

Recently, the same organization wrote:

> Defining charter schools is difficult because state laws that govern them *are so different* (author's emphasis). However, charter schools generally share three characteristics:
>
> - They are public schools—free to attend, publicly funded, part of the state school system, and accountable to public bodies[2] for their results.
> - They are schools of choice, so they do not enroll students solely based on where they live.
> - They are privately managed by an organization that has a charter, or contract, with a charter authorizer.[3]

The stated intentions sound innocuous enough.

After more than a quarter of a century of charter experimentation, this work asks, "What are the results of this application of an economic theory of action to a public good?"

Joseph Heller's novel, *Something Happened*, is the story of a marriage that has gone south because the married couple *was not paying attention to what was going on in their relationship* (Heller, 1974). The characters in that story realize that something has happened, but they are powerless to fully understand and change the outcome[4] toward which they are heading.

Something has happened to American public education. We need to pay attention.

Our children, as in any divorce, will suffer harm from our lack of attention to our commitments to one another in a democratic republic. This observation does not only apply to our schools. Our levels of civic engagement have fallen off dramatically in the late twentieth and now in the twenty-first centuries. The loss of social capital researched and noted by Robert Putnam in *Bowling Alone* is continuing (Putnam, 2000).

Like the frog in the water that is gradually being heated up to boiling, we are not paying attention to the consequences of our "choices" regarding our public schools. We are unconsciously musing to ourselves, *Hey, this school choice water feels pretty good, a lot better than when I could only pick the local pond where I was born.*

We are missing the signs that the local pond where the tadpoles came from and where we learned how to swim is being drained. When it dries up, we can't return "home."

Public schools define our communities and who we are. The home team is the team that wears the local high school's colors under the Friday night lights. Those lights are being dimmed.

We have allowed something to happen to the way we provide an American education to our children. Something happened between 1991 and the present day.

If we do not become focally aware of what is actually going on during this phase one of privatizing our schools, phase two, in which parents pay for their children's education, will surely follow. Our social contract with, and our moral commitments to, *one another* will be irreparably damaged.

"Catch 22" was Joseph Heller's take on the Army Air Corps' rule that in order to report yourself as insane you must be sane, a form of circular reasoning. Circular reasoning is present in the arguments used to defend current financial practices *in both districts and the choice marketplaces*. The results are insanity at both types of "public" schools.

Rather than rely on partisan statistics from pro- and anti-charter school advocacy groups, a new collation of fiscal data drawn from audits, annual financial reviews, and IRS filings was used to analyze the effects of this economic model on the governance and financing of charter schools.

A forensic accounting approach was used during the research phase of this work. Forensic accounting helps to clearly delineate and show who is choosing and who is losing in this new consumer model-driven deal. There are elements of the financial results exposed that rightfully appall thoughtful citizens of our republic from both sides of the aisle. If we read the original thesis justifying this arrangement to contract out education, its *true intentions* become clear.

Ed Choice, a charter advocacy group, to its credit, places a part of Milton Friedman's choice argument[5] on its webpage and includes an important endnote from Dr. Friedman regarding financing education. A link to the source is provided in the footnotes.

The separation of a child from a parent who cannot pay for the minimum required education is clearly inconsistent with our reliance on the family as the basic social unit and our belief in the freedom of the individual. Yet, even so, if the financial burden imposed by such an educational requirement could readily be met by the great bulk of the families in a community, *it might be both feasible and desirable to require the parents to meet the cost directly.*

Extreme cases could be handled by special provisions in much the same way as is done now for housing and automobiles. An even closer analogy is provided by present arrangements for children who are mistreated by their parents. *The advantage of imposing the costs on the parents is that it would tend to equalize the social and private costs of having children and so promote a better distribution of families by size.*

The following footnote from the original *Capitalism and Freedom* is given at the end of the page (Friedman, 1962, p. 37).

It is by no means as fantastic[6] as may appear that such a step would noticeably affect the size of families. For example, one explanation of the lower birthrate among higher than among lower socio-economic groups may well be that children are relatively more expensive to the former thanks in considerable measure to the higher standards of schooling they maintain, the costs of which they bear.

The meaning? If families are forced to pay for the cost of a child's education in a democratic republic, then they will choose to have fewer children, like the higher socioeconomic groups in the 1960s that sent their children to private school.

The model also predicted that eventually choice would lead to a stronger middle class and less of a concentration of wealth as that middle class moved up the social ladder. This in turn would allow more people the option of paying for their children's education. After twenty-five years of experimenting, that economic gap has become wider.

We've been here before. We had periods in our history when paying for a child's education *was the parents' responsibility.* We also allowed children to work ten- to twelve-hour days in factories and mines at the time.

The antithesis of the assumption in Friedman's argument was seen in poor families prior to child labor laws.[7] Having lots of children was employed then as a way those families could make ends meet—by putting those children to work. In today's world, where the economic model for most families has both parents working two and sometimes three jobs to make ends meet, is this really where we want to head?

The term *American education* is used throughout this work because the guiding principle of the educational philosophies that drove the republic's movement to compulsory education laws has always been focused on preparing students for a life as participating citizens of a democratic republic, a process known as acculturation.

Part of that acculturation process is ensuring we pass on the current state of our union rather than a version of the "good old days."

The child labor laws were designed to open up educational opportunities to all children by limiting the number of hours a child under the age of sixteen could work.

Child labor laws[8] ultimately established the need for the U.S. Department of Labor:

> *The most sweeping federal law that restricts the employment and abuse of child workers is the Fair Labor Standards Act (FLSA).*[9] *Child labor provisions under FLSA are designed to protect the educational opportunities of youth and prohibit their employment in jobs that are detrimental to their health and safety.*

The teaching profession, which has always been under attack for its affiliation with the AFT or NEA, is experiencing a frontal assault that questions the value of teaching as a profession while it attacks the ability of teachers to organize into labor unions.

The effects of right to work laws on teacher compensation and benefits are clear. Teachers at charters receive work agreements instead of contracts. Several conversations with major charter holders regarding their system of compensation and employment benefits for teachers elicited this response: "*Most of our teachers are short term. They are teaching prior to going into their real profession or at the end of another professional life. We don't participate in the retirement system but we provide a match of up to 6% which they can take with them when they leave.*"

Statistics on staff turnover at charters validate this statement's accuracy.

The profession is becoming de-professionalized.

NOTES

1, In fiscal year 2017, 35 percent of charter schools were not rated by the Arizona Department of Education. Online schools, small schools, and alternative schools were treated this way. The online school with the largest population of Arizona students was unrated. The owner took an $8M-plus distribution in that year.

2. In the majority of states with charter laws on the books, these bodies are public, but they are unelected. Their meetings are subject to the open meeting laws; however, the monitoring of compliance with this rule is limited.

3, http://www.ncsl.org/research/education/charter-schools-overview.aspx.

4. At this point, the data GCI has indicated that there is nothing that can be done to save a portion of the charters that will eventually collapse financially. The data can

be used to ensure that the failure does not happen during the school year, disrupting children's lives and leaving parents in the lurch.

5. https://www.edchoice.org/who-we-are/our-founders/the-friedmans-on-school-choice/article/the-role-of-government-in-education/.

6. The original quote uses "so" rather than "as." The expression has gone out of style since Dr. Friedman used it.

7. These date to the same period as compulsory education.

8. https://www.dol.gov/general/topic/youthlabor.

9. https://www.dol.gov/whd/flsa/.

Chapter Four

De-professionalizing American Public Education

During the spring of 2018, teachers in Arizona, Oklahoma, and West Virginia took to the streets to protest educational funding in their states. In 2019, teachers in California and Colorado have followed suit. The central issue in these states was teacher pay, which was close to the lowest in the nation in Arizona, Oklahoma, and West Virginia.

Voter initiatives to increase teachers' pay in the past have been blocked or modified by the legislature in Arizona and other states. In Arizona, Proposition 100, Performance Pay Initiative Proposition 301 (funded by an increase in the state's sales tax) and a proposition to restrict further expansion of voucher programs, Proposition 305, were a clear message that voters supported their teachers and expected public schools and public charter schools *to fulfill their wishes by compensating their teachers and restricting private placement paid for by the state.*

Proposition 305 specifically limited the expansion of voucher programs, an initiative that was organized by parents under the banner of a coalition of parents known as "Save our Schools."

When voters support their public schools, they are implicitly and explicitly supporting their public school teachers, and by extension charter school teachers. Voters from both sides of the aisle expect that with additional funding comes accountability for spending. This public expectation is being sidestepped and ignored by state legislators who are intent on expanding "school choice."

There is a reason why right to work laws usually precede the establishment of charters in states that have legislated this market sector into business. Controlling unions, especially teacher unions, is another element of the economic free-market theory behind charter schools and vouchers. Right to work laws are a form of union busting.

In preparing the "market" for competition for high-quality teachers, a theory of high-performing teachers becoming highly compensated was put into the privatization arguments.

The original arguments for charters discussed teacher salaries in an "open market" competing for highly effective teachers, the result of multiple charter school and private school owners seeking out the "best teachers."

Salaries of $100,000 were predicted for teachers who, at the time this claim was made in the early 1970s, were making well under $10,000.[1] The theory also predicted that teachers who were incompetent or ineffective would be eliminated from the labor pool when the obstacles preventing their removal were removed.[2] This false claim is part of a general trend to repeal or neutralize our hard-won labor laws.

Milton Friedman said:

With respect to teachers' salaries . . . poor teachers are grossly overpaid and good teachers grossly underpaid. Salary schedules tend to be uniform and determined far more by seniority.

REPEALING LABOR LAWS

The National Institute for Labor Relations Research along with Leaders and members of the National Right to Work Committee advocates for the repeal of the provisions in the National Labor Relations Act (NLRA) and other federal statutes that force employers to recognize a union supported by a majority of front-line employees as the monopoly-bargaining agent of all such employees, including those who oppose unionization and would never voluntarily join a union. Right to Work leaders have also indicated that simply repealing the NLRA, without replacing it with any other federal labor statute, would be a worthy endeavor. Libertarians overwhelmingly concur.[3]

In their own words, this organization calls for a repeal of *all federal labor statutes*. The same laws that eliminated child labor in the "free market" would go away, with the free market taking over in their stead.

A reading of Sinclair Lewis's works and those of Charles Dickens might be a good place for these free marketers to start to ground their "innovative ideas" in reality. These ideas have been tried; they failed. Even Scrooge eventually came to his senses. As citizens we need to heed the warnings embedded in the theories behind privatization of our educational systems. What is the next privatization market, public fire and police departments?

Equally insidious are the stated reasons given by charter school advocacy groups for paying teachers less and not funding a pension plan for their teachers. These include statements that equate teaching with a stop on the professional career path of a college graduate in any field. That is, there is an assumption that they will only be teachers for three to five years. After that they will join the free-market workforce. This three- to five-year figure is remarkably close to the turnover rate at charters.

We can't absorb this type of loss to the teacher labor pool. Currently the nation is experiencing a teacher shortage of approximately 20 percent. Teaching jobs are being filled by uncertified practitioners in some of our most crucial subject areas, mathematics and science. The market can't bear salaries that do not reflect the market value of those teachers' services.

It is time to reexamine what has been wrought by a deregulated privatization of a public good based on an economic theory of action. Pat answers such as "We are running schools like a business" are often the response when charter advocates and businesses respond to critiques of their model in the press.

We ask, "What type of business are you really running because the financial data is not adding up?" The losers in this mix of business and education appear to be teachers and students. Charter school teachers earn about 20 percent less than their public school colleagues.

Only 42 percent of charters provide access to state retirement systems for teachers, and benefits beyond the retirement system lag behind comparable benefits in the "free-market" professions (the highest benefit percentage seen in the data was 27 percent, with lows that reflected only FICA and Medicare payments by the provider).

Corporate mindsets seek to maximize profits while limiting employee compensation and spending. In a state where teachers are already among the lowest paid in the country, there remains a significant gap between teacher compensation in the districts versus teachers employed by charters.

The following table shows that this lag in spending on teacher compensation is also present in special education expenditures.

Special education expenditures in the districts represent 12 percent of all expenditures, while charters spend only 5 percent of their funding on special needs students.

The 2014 Annual Report of the Arizona Superintendent for Public Instruction showed that charter schools spent 45 percent of revenues on classroom expenditures versus district spending in the same area of 52 percent. In fiscal year 2017, the statistics were 46.6 percent in charter schools versus 51.66 percent in the districts. *Money spent on actually educating students is a loser when economics drive decision making.*

When confronted with this disparity, privatizers respond with a strange but telling logic. They contend that by leasing their employees, they can avoid the costs of the state's retirement system, so therefore the personnel costs (area 1000 on the budget) go down. This, we are told, is because the company

Table 4.1. Teacher Compensation and SPED Expenditures as of June 30, 2017, in Arizona Districts

		Total District ADM 926,354.21
Year-End District Teacher Count Full-Time Equivalent FTE	49,625.20	
Year-End District Teacher Salaries All	$2,441,886,153	
	$49,206.58	Average Pay FTEs
Special Education as a Percentage of Expenditures	12.15%	
Same Data for Arizona Charters		Total Charter ADM 179,669.18
Year-End Charter Teacher Full-Time Equivalent FTE	9,950.30	
Year-End Charter Teacher Salaries All	$408,622,730	
	$41,066.37	Average Pay FTEs
Salary Compared to District Average	83.46% of District Average	
Special Education as a Percentage of Expenditures Actual % Spent	4.94%	
SPED Expenditures compared to a District	40.67% of District Spending on SPED	

Source: 2017 Superintendent's Report AZDOE

saved money and created efficiencies for training new staff and managing personnel.

This seems to make sense; however, if some of those savings went to compensating their teachers rather than to profit from the 12 percent drop in teacher-related expenses, the bottom line in the personnel account would remain static. That is, it would not reflect a 6 to 7 percent difference from personnel costs posted by the "competitor" district.

Special education expenditures, which are also delineated on the annual superintendent's report,[4] showed that districts were spending 12.15 percent of their budget on special education while charters were spending 4.94 percent of their budgets on their special education students. Special education is a loser by almost three to one when economics, not special education plans, drive decision making.

Either charters are discouraging special education students from attending, or they are shirking their duty to meet these children's educational needs. An almost three-to-one gap in spending is a "tell" that something is amiss.

TAKE CARE OF BUSINESS

Current financial practices by most charters fall short of sound business financial standards and the public's expectations as to how their educational dollars are being spent (Bennis, Parikh, & Lessem, 1994; Dewey, 1891; Knight & Friedman, 1935; Pojman, Vaughn, & Vaughn, 2014). Greater flexibility regarding spending decisions has not led to better academic results: Two independent studies found that demographically similar students[5] did just as well or better on average in public district schools. In Arizona, 35 percent of charters were not rated on the "A through F" standards in FY 2018, including all of the online schools.

One thing is certain: When the public votes to increase expenditures for our public schools, one of their intentions is to ensure that their teachers are paid a living wage. This is part of the social agreement between a community and its teachers. Charters and private school contractors paying their teachers 15 to 20 percent less than district teachers and eliminating benefits for their teachers violates that social contract.

Notably, 23 percent of charters are providing the opportunities promised in charter legislation. These are that rare breed of charter owners who do not need additional oversight to do the right thing. Two large charters that are exemplars of this type of organization are the Arizona Agribusiness and Equine Center and Northland Preparatory. These are the type of charters that should be emulated and replicated. Their business models are financially sound and ethical. These charter champions also treat their teachers as professionals. It can be done.

With business CEOs in charters receiving compensation packages and investment incomes in the millions (all legal under charter law), we ask this of the economic model in place: How has the business model for educational services worked out?

Schooling is occurring in a business model in which educational outcomes are supposed to be guaranteed by free-market choices. The results have been the same type of free market, deregulated, financial malaise seen in other deregulated businesses in the recent past. This is not what the noble experiment of public education was set up to do.

What was that noble experiment? To promote the public good. Real educational choice does that.

NOTES

1. The author started his career in New Hampshire at a salary of $6,800 per year in 1974. The district also provided the State Retirement System funding and a full medical and dental plan.

2. This theory ignored pre-union days' data that pointed to long-term teachers being eliminated because they cost more. As an administrator in public districts and charters, I never experienced union opposition to the termination of an incompetent teacher, as long as due process was given to that teacher. As an administrator in charter schools, it was difficult to release friends and family of the charter holder. Who is more difficult to fire for incompetence?

3. http://www.nilrr.org/.

4. Data compiled from Annual Superintendent's Reports from FY 2014 through FY 2017. Under 94.142 the LEA designated as the responsible party for serious special educational students is the local district.

5. See *Carpetbagging America's Public Schools* or Grand Canyon Institutes' Following the Money Report, available at www.grandcanyoninstitute.org for no cost. These reports are analyzed in both of these documents.

Chapter Five

What about the Sermon on the Mount?

When confronted by hostile questions about his writing's cynicism regarding unbridled capitalism, Kurt Vonnegut often asked this question of the inquisitor: "What about the Sermon on the Mount, sir?"

Money, riches, and an unbridled quest for the "good life" can distract us from achieving what social responsibility and our duty to one another as citizens of this republic compel us to believe regarding right and wrong. The love of money corrupts us to the point where we become indifferent to what is right and what is wrong. We know instinctively that power corrupts and that absolute power corrupts absolutely.

The state and federal legislation regarding charters and vouchers is a calculated undermining and replacement (or usurping) of locally controlled public education. The privatization effort is sardonically referred to as "starving the beast of public education" by politicians whose main concern is often the cost, not the quality, of public education. We have opened Pandora's box, removed the hinges, and thrown away the key.

Ironically, the data reveals that financial malaise is plaguing the charter industry. It costs *the state* more to fund a charter or private placement than it does to fund the same student at their local schools. Charter lobbyists continue to press legislatures for more and more state funding, and they sometimes have the audacity to go after local funding for their business ventures.

Charter authorizers are state-appointed agencies, not locally elected school boards. This governance model effectively emancipates the charter business contractor from any local fiscal oversight. This work will show that this effort is part of a political and economic strategic goal of privatizing public education services in the United States.

Privatizers have confused our economic system, capitalism, with our political system, which is a democratic republic whose stated goal is liberty and justice for all.

Is that really what we, the citizens of this republic, want from our public investment in our public schools?

We have had privatized education before. How did that work out?

Chapter Six

The Good Old Days

In the years before tax-funded public education, all parents were responsible for funding their children's education. We are heading back to those "good old days." Parents had a Hobson's choice in the good old days prior to the availability of a free and appropriate public education. They could pay for a private education or, as most did, keep their children out of school—a true free-market, economics-driven choice.

As a nation, we have been here before.

Public common schools were initiated to ensure that all of our citizens had an opportunity to attend school. Liberty and justice for all meant that all of America's children deserved an American education that prepared them for life in a democratic republic.

The current model of education as a contracted service is not working. It is, as is any choice that separates children in our community, "unlovely and a threat to our democracy." This doesn't have to be the case. It is also not what the founders envisioned public education looking like in a republic.

In a letter[1] to John Adams, Thomas Jefferson wrote about the idea of entrusting education to the "free-market" schools at the time. Jefferson hoped we would sober up and see the folly of this approach in the future.

> When sobered by experience I hope our successors will turn their attention to the advantages of education. I mean of education on the broad scale, and not that of the petty academies, as they call themselves, which are starting up in every neighborhood, and where one or two men, possessing Latin, and sometimes Greek, a knowledge of the globes, and the first six books of Euclid, imagine and communicate this as the sum of science. *They commit their pupils to the theatre*

of the world with just taste enough of learning to be alienated from industrious pursuits, and not enough to do service in the ranks of science.

In the data on charter schools, there are charter owners and charter companies that understand that charter schools are more than private businesses operating for profit alone. *Charters and districts that remain centered on their commitment to a community of learners get this right. We should applaud and support their efforts and commitment.*

As an early adopter of the charter model, the author knows the difficulties and sacrifice that these charter exemplars (statistically 23 percent of the market) go through to make this happen. These charter champions deserve a universal choice model based on Dr. Budde's, Horace Mann's, and John Dewey's original ideals for a free and appropriate publicly funded education. They remain focused on the primary mission of an American public education: the education of American citizens as members of a democratic republic.

Who is choosing and who is losing in this economic theory applied wholesale to public education?

We, as members of a free society, have always had freedom over our educational choices. With that freedom came responsibility. Our civic responsibility to each other to provide a public education for all of our children was succinctly stated by John Dewey: "What the best and wisest parent wants for his child, that must we want for all the children of the community. Any other ideal for our schools is narrow and unlovely, acted upon it destroys our democracy."

Dewey chose the words "*our schools*" for a reason.

Common schools were meant to provide for the common good, not to pay for private placements at private properties based on a consumer choice.

Calling this a "freedom to choose" is a play on words and our viler, self-serving instincts to look out for ourselves first.

Deep down, we know from our upbringing that freedom is not free. The better angels of our nature know that this arrangement is not drawing us together as citizens of a republic. We are drifting further apart. The glue that binds us to our community and to one another is being dissolved one choice at a time.

We have forgotten that with great freedom comes great responsibility. In a democratic republic, we are our brother's keepers.

As our teachers have often stated, "We can do better, if only we apply ourselves."

As citizens in a democratic republic, we need to choose wisely. Financial responsibility comes with economic choices. The two cannot be separated.

Even Milton Friedman, the architect of the current choice model, knew: "There is no such thing as a free lunch" (1975). The price for this free lunch has been lost in financial, political, and social capital in our communities. These are the costs of schooling alone.

NOTE

1. For the entire letter, see http://www.let.rug.nl/usa/presidents/thomas-jefferson/letters-of-thomas-jefferson/jefl231.php.

Chapter Seven

Public or Private?

Charter schools are "public schools of choice" in one sense only. Charter schools' contracts and vouchers *are paid for with publicly raised funding (taxes) from the state and federal governments.*

In most states, those funds come from equalized valuation formulas[1] that were the result of local communities in the state banding together and suing the individual states for a funding redistribution model for state educational revenues. The formulas were based on a community's ability to raise taxes on local property to support its schools. These cases were litigated during the last half of the last century.

The result was the Equalized Valuation Funding formulas, called by various names in each state. The local community then supplemented those state funds with local and county tax revenues (property taxes) to pay for their public schools.

Local *control* of public education was sacrosanct.

The assumption in the choice model is that taxpayer-funded money to support public education from the state belongs to the individual "consumer of educational services."

That consumer now has a publicly funded "choice." Once that tax-sourced money is paid to the contractor, it then becomes (according to the model) the financial capital of the contractors to use as they see fit. The "freedom to choose" model is based on a capitalist economic theory of action applied to a tax-funded public good. An oxymoron.

The funding from the state reflects the full amount that the state pays in the poorest districts plus any extra funding provided in law (currently—in 2018—an additional $2,000-plus in Arizona).

A student choosing to attend a charter in a property-rich town *gets the same state funding as a student attending the poorest school district in the state.*

The equalization formula, hard fought for by local governments and school boards, goes out the door. The equalization[2] of funding based on a community's ability to pay for education in that community has been cancelled out in this transaction.

School choice *is not a zero sum* revenue game for district schools.

Choice costs states more because *we are now funding choices that once were the financial responsibility of the parents electing to make that consumer choice.* States are also supplying a full ADM share to children attending a charter within a district that may receive only a partial ADM share under Equalized Educational Funding.

The property and assets in half of the states surveyed are not a part of this contractual *arrangement*. In states that allow private ownership of the assets, the educational contract is for the child's education, *not the school buildings and assets.* This in spite of the fact that many of those states provide extra funding beyond the allocation from Equalized Valuation Revenues[3] *specifically for the purpose of obtaining property and maintaining those private properties.*

There are, as one might expect, exceptions from state to state.

In several states, charters are also authorized to seek a portion of the locally raised funding for public school buildings. In those states, the local school board typically retains its fiscal oversight over the contracted, privately held charter.

Twenty-one states *do not allow* the charter holder to own the property acquired with charter contract allocations. Those states receive low "choice friendliness" scores from the charter advocacy groups that monitor the legislation enabling charter schools across the country. The fact is that many are in the charter business as a means to game the school real estate market.

There are wide variances in different states' charter authorizing laws, with seven states opting out of chartering altogether as of 2018.

Vouchers for scholarships to private schools represent another privatization of our tax-funded capital expenditures for education. Another "free-market" business has sprung up dealing with tax credit scholarships to religious and other types of private schools. The financial capital from tax credits to individuals and businesses for donations to these "scholarships" is paid out to *contracted education scholarship vendors*. Parents apply to these scholarship vendors for access to the funds accumulated by the vendor from tax credit "donations" from individuals and businesses.

The operating economic theory is that once the money is paid out on behalf of the parents to the private school scholarship contractor, the contractors are free to distribute it as they see fit to private schools with which they are affiliated.

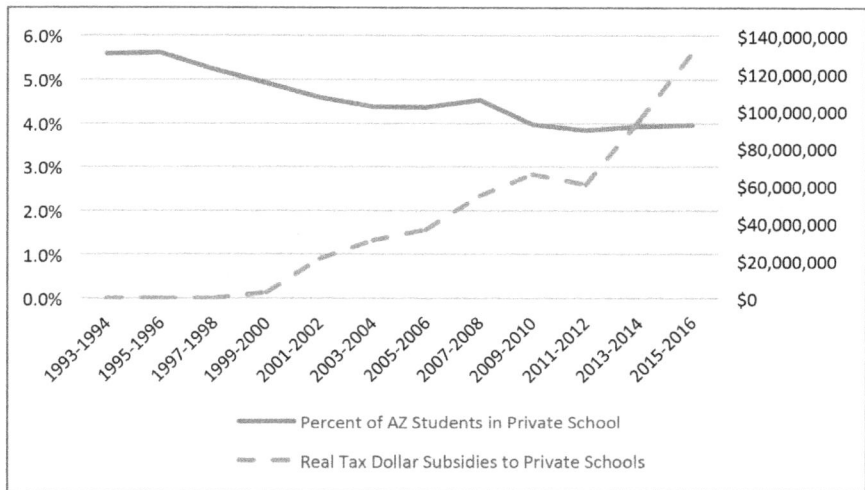

Figure 7.1. Growing Tax Subsidies to Private Schools in Arizona
Source: Grand Canyon Institute Report. See www.grandcanyoninstitute.org.

Tax credits, as opposed to tax deductions, for corporations and individuals allow the funding of scholarships for individual students at private and religious-oriented schools with a tax credit going to the donor. Fiscal year 2018 data shows that 55 percent of these "scholarships" were earmarked for various religious schools.

A private scholarship market has sprung up to take advantage of this new "economic opportunity." The scholarship distributors[4] are privately held clearinghouses that distribute the scholarships while taking 10 to 15 percent of the gross revenues of the organization as their "free-market profit."

If you have the right connections, you can apply for several "scholarships." Research by the Grand Canyon Institute's Dr. David Wells shows that the average total scholarship[5] is $10,700, as of FY 2016, a substantial amount above the state's equalized valuation payments, with additional funding included, to a charter school.

The number of recipients of these scholarships has actually declined. The funds that were "donated" to these funds come from tax credits, which, unlike a tax deduction, decrease the state's revenue stream dollar for dollar.

Most of the forty-four states with charter laws exempt the CEOs holding the charter and opportunity scholarship companies from the normal financial rules regarding nepotism, contract bidding, and self-dealing with related party firms controlled by the same CEO and corporate board or relatives.

The rules that guide our public, school board-governed district schools have been purposely deregulated for the charter and voucher sectors of this "competitive" market. The charter industry claims this is just like other state contracts for services. *It isn't.*

The rules of this contract services market *do not conform to normal state contracting agreements with private companies,, such as road construction contracts with construction companies.*

Charter contracts are designed to leave the contractor in a position to legally spend the money received from tax sources on related party contracts with subsidiaries of the charter. Unlike construction contractors to the state, those charter sub-contracts can be with another company owned by the charter holder and related party subsidiaries. These subsidiaries are often held by the same corporate board and management team.

This use of related party transactions and related party labor is the case at 95 percent of charter schools in the data. Charter contractors, unlike road contractors, do not have to prove to the authorizer or the state that they are financially able to complete the contract, that is, that they can deliver on the contract. They also don't have to list those sub-contractors' financials.

When a charter contractor closes their school down during the school year, as eighty-two sites in Arizona have done,[6] the state is unable to recover the money it spent on a full year of educational services. The state also has no claim or stake on the failed charter's assets. Those assets go to the bondholders. The normal rules governing educational spending have been *deregulated*.

A recent guest article in the *Arizona Republic* written by an Arizona charter owner, State Senator Eddie Farnsworth, a long-term Arizona legislator, defended this type of contracting. He chose the interesting position of stating that these types of related party transactions are the case at 95 percent of charter schools.

Mr. Farnsworth's 95 percent figure is correct. That figure correlates to the number of charters that sought this variance from the state charter board, that is, to use related party contractors.

The data used in this treatise eliminated those related party transactions that were actually "saving money and creating efficiencies" *for their educational programs* by the use of these legally authorized transactions (23 percent of all cases). These charter holders are exemplars in the data. This work will highlight these types of charters as models.

In contrast, 77 percent of the related party transactions in our data did not save money or create efficiencies. They were designed to siphon off funds to *non-school-related party entities*. The algorithm[7] for this analysis has been published and is available at the websites listed in the endnotes. Related party

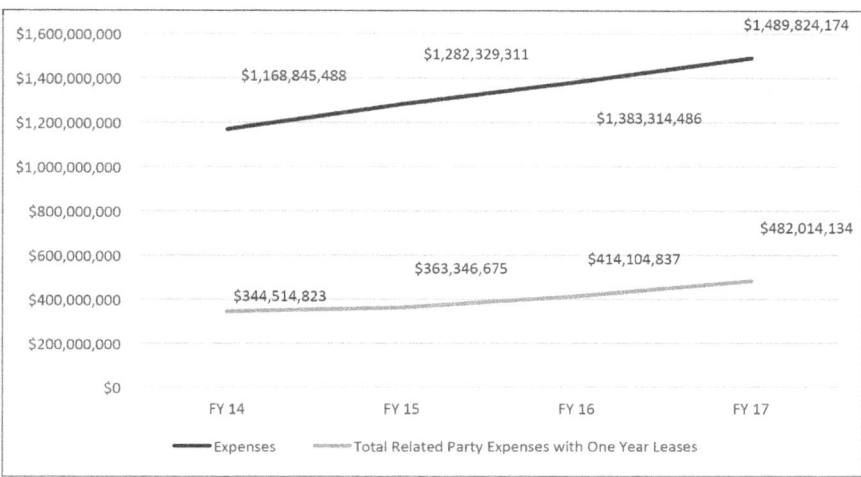

Figure 7.2. Total Expenses to Total Related Party Expenses

expenses at charters as compared to their total expenses are illustrated in the graph above.

Our historic commitment to a public education provided by our local communities is slowly being starved off and replaced by state-authorized private educational service providers. Increasingly the transactions involved are concentrated in ever smaller circles of insiders, choking off the economic benefits of public education spending in our communities.

As citizens in a democratic republic, we need to be focally aware of the consequences of our choices and the societal costs of those choices on the common good. Public education, teachers, and local school boards are enduring a death by a thousand cuts. Our duty and obligation as citizens to provide a "free and appropriate" public education for our children is being subcontracted out to private schools and privately owned charter corporations.

As a result of privatization, communities' economic, social, and political capital is being compromised and destroyed, as we, the new "consumers of educational services," choose to school alone outside of our local public school system.

A new form of self-selected segregation of our children by academic performance, religion, and socioeconomic grouping results in lost economic, political, and social capital in our communities. Contracted privatization is becoming the new educational funding norm.

As noted, this is not a zero-sum game. When we "choose" for our child, someone else's child loses. The current choice model is inconsistent with the theory of justice proposed by Rawls (1971). Liberty and justice for all, as we recite in the Pledge of Allegiance daily in our public schools, is being compromised. The loss is measurable in the data showing lost financial resources and the data on financial malaise at privately held charter and private schools.

More importantly, the social and political capital of our community is diminished.

These types of losses are a threat to our democracy. We remove our loyalty, and more importantly, our voice, from our public schools when we choose to exit those community schools and school alone.

We are no longer being true to *our* school. We have become true to a privately held school paid for by a state government subsidy.

Those schools aren't really ours.

They are owned by a company that may be owned by a conglomerate from another state or another country, not the community in which they are located. Where those companies located their business is the result of a business decision, not a community decision based on the community's educational needs. The simple conversations that make up our involvement with our community and with one another are interrupted when we choose to school alone (Wheatley, 2002).

Civic engagement has dropped dramatically at the local level since the mid-1960s. The social capital losses noted in Robert Putnam's *Bowling Alone* are being magnified because our state legislators have encouraged, with their legislative actions, our citizens to school alone.

A "free-market" economic theory is gradually, and deliberately, being substituted for a locally controlled and governed neighborhood school system.

Education in this model *is now treated as a contracted purchased service*, not a community-based *direct service* to the community's education of its children.

The administrators and teachers at charters and private schools are employees of the educational contractor. They do not, by definition, work for the public. They work for a private contractor whose contract is with the state and monitored by the state's charter authorizing agencies.

The social circle of the community has been supplanted by a corporate entity promising us new "choices."

It is not a coincidence that once public schools and communities widened their schools' circle to include all races, creeds, and abilities, the impetus driving the voucher and charter movements was born. This twenty-five-year-long-plus experiment in providing government funding for privatized "public" educational services has a direct effect on the financial capital we provide as citizens to educate our children.

The true nature of this model reveals itself in financial transactions hidden from the public's eye and local oversight. From a strictly business perspective, the picture is unlovely and a clear and present danger to how we fund education. The model, like the mortgage lending model of the deregulated early 2000s, is breaking the bank.

More important than the financial costs, this work analyzes how this new set of deregulated rules disrupts and depletes local political and social capital as the nation moves closer and closer to schooling alone.[8] We are choosing our way to government-subsidized isolation from other citizens in our communities.

Dr. Budde's disruptive innovation, which maintained this community link, has morphed into a destructive innovation. It is destroying our sense of *community purpose* and unity with our fellow citizens.

This radical redefinition and reconstruction of what constitutes legitimate public education expenditure in a republic has been in place since 1991.

We have all heard the expression that possession is nine-tenths of the law. The laws in those states that allow for private ownership of "public" schools are clear. We, the public, *do not own the charter school contractor's school property and assets*. They are not "our schools."

Decision making regarding how money is spent and what is taught, the curriculum, belongs to the charter holders in possession of the school buildings and assets, *not the community*.

Enlightened charter holders, the real innovators in the mix, who keep the public in their public schools, have become disenchanted and disgusted with this hostile corporate takeover of America's public schools. Their voice is also present in this work.

NOTES

1. Equalized Valuation is a formula used to determine a community's real estate assets relating the total sum to the amount that that community can afford to pay for its schools. Equalization is a method that equalizes all state aid for local schools based on a community's ability to pay. Scottsdale, a relatively wealthy community, gets little to no state aid for in-district students. A child electing to go to school in a Scottsdale charter school gets a full Equalized Revenue payment while a student from another district electing to go to a Scottsdale district school is paid for in the normal way that Scottsdale covers in-district students: that is, that student's tuition is on the Scottsdale taxpayers. This is a consequence of open in enrollment, which is an unfunded mandate.

2. Contradicting this funding logic is the fact that a student "choosing" to attend Scottsdale schools from a poor district school does not bring the added state revenue

that a charter student would bring in their charter "backpacks full of cash." This matters financially, as charters and private schools typically pick locations where their economic success and academic success are likely to be guaranteed by the area's socioeconomic strengths. Businesses know that location is a key factor in determining their success in a competitive market. Open enrollment, which typically precedes chartering laws, places the financial burden caused by that out-of-district choice on the local community accepting the student. This lack of funding for an inter-district choice represents an unfunded mandate.

3. Equalized Valuation formulas are the result of past legal challenges to state funding of education. Formulas determine which districts get full funding and which districts receive less or no funding from the state, based on the community's ability to raise taxes on taxable properties. Charter contractors receive full funding from the state no matter where the charter is located in the state, and in the case of extra funding, additional funds for leases and property acquisition. Theoretically, this extra funding is to offset the fact that districts can tax local property to fund their buildings. In a district, the community owns those properties.

4. Related party transactions are also permissible in this scholarship marketplace, a topic covered in *The Carpetbagging of America's Public Schools*, published by Rowman and Littlefield (2018).

5. Source: http://grandcanyoninstitute.org/10700-per-student-the-estimated-cost-of-arizonas-private-school-subsidy-programs/.

6. In Milwaukee, where vouchers for private schools were initiated, 41 percent of the private schools that sprang up have been shuttered as of FY 2016. See http://weac.org/2016/06/16/researcher-stunned-by-high-rate-of-voucher-school-failures-in-milwaukee/.

7. See www.grandcanyoninstitute.org. See the paper "Following the Money" at http://grandcanyoninstitute.org/following-the-money-twenty-years-of-charter-school-finances-in-arizona/.

8. Schooling alone is especially insidious when we opt for an online-only program in which the child's entire experience of "public" school is done at home on a computer. These programs also tend to represent the highest profiteering levels in the charter industry.

Chapter Eight

A Contracted Service

The current charter governance model for charter schools is the antithesis of where Dr. Budde's charter model indicated this locus of control should be centered, that is, locally. An offer we could not refuse of "freedom of choice" has led to a contracted service model with private companies. This has been sold as a way to personalize public education for our children.

It's not personal; it's business.

The author became an early believer in Dr. Budde's model while listening to those ideas at the University of Massachusetts in the early seventies. As a newly minted superintendent in 1999, the author administered a New Hampshire school district that was one of the limited number of USDOE Public School Charter grants made in 2000. The purpose of that five-year, $12.5 million grant was to provide innovative educational options within the public school system, run by teachers from the district who wanted to explore educational choices for their students.

To pass muster with the grant authorizer, USDOE, the charter choices had to be significantly *different from* the offerings at the existing public schools. Those choices were designed to supplement our existing choices. They were not designed to supplant the primary means of delivering an education to our students. The federal grant provided the funding that was used to start charter programs *without financially impacting the primary means of providing education in our local schools.*

The grant involved a cooperative effort among all of the districts, universities, and state colleges in the southwestern corner of New Hampshire. This required multiple open meetings with the parents and students in those communities. Our model included an open enrollment policy allowing students from one district to attend another district's schools. The area's need for different types of educational options was assessed with the public prior to applying for and receiving this grant. Local businesses and charities funded the planning and the startup costs.

Since those starry-eyed days, and after over a decade of experience in the charter and voucher "market sector," my mindset has changed. The validity and viability of the economic theory and contracting that underpin the current version of the charter "choice" model is nothing like what Dr. Budde's vision called for.

The charter industry has co-opted parts of the originator's language into their descriptions of "public charter schools" while gutting the spirit of Dr. Budde's governance model. When you ask the public what they want regarding choices, their first answer is not privatization. The communities[1] that backed our charter initiative in New Hampshire specifically stated that charters were to *supplement, not supplant* the locally controlled[2] educational programs in the Monadnock Region.

The finances of our chartering and schools-within-schools efforts were controlled by a third party, Antioch New England, with fiscal monitoring bolstered by a district-level business manager who reported the financial data to all three districts and the universities involved in the grant.

The disappointments with how charter schools have evolved in this country are reflected in practitioners' comments in the introduction and within this work. This disappointment *has not led the majority of those charter innovators to give up on the idea of public charter schools.*

Reflective practitioners will always acknowledge that there are also issues in public schools that need correcting. However, the real innovators in the charter movement are tired of the realities of an economic theory of action driving the "charter marketplace."

This disappointment is voiced almost daily in articles published across the country. Anne Dichele's voice is an example of the chagrin and disappointment that our most innovative educators are feeling regarding the privatization version of the choice model.

Anne Dichele opened her charter during the early years of charter schools in Connecticut. The reality of "allowing the camel to get his nose in the tent" led her to write this piece, used with her permission, regarding charter management corporations and publish it in the *Hartford Current*:

> As one of the founders and board chair of a small charter school in Connecticut, I am more and more dismayed at the state of the once-admirable charter school movement in this country.
>
> In 1997, Side by Side Charter School in Norwalk opened its doors—the first of only 12 charter schools in Connecticut. I and the six other founders met every weekend for the two years prior to the opening to design an overall plan for a school that we were not sure would come to fruition. The application process

was extensive and overwhelming. So when our dream of opening a school that was big on innovation and small on red tape was approved, we were thrilled.

Twenty years have passed. We have not sought to grow larger, to build bigger or to become a franchise of successful schools. Why? Because our mission was never to become a corporation for education, a for-profit enterprise, an organization that promulgated a tidy panacea for solving educational problems. What we are is what we always intended—a school that practices innovative ideas; ideas that are research-based and promote student success. We are a haven for students who, though disenfranchised economically and socially, are taught to understand their important role in a democracy, to question structural inequities and develop the writing, reading, speaking and critical thinking skills that all schools should provide.

We took seriously that our successes (we are now the top performing charter school in the state by school performance measures) are to be shared but not necessarily replicated. Rather than build a corporation, we have chosen to build a beacon of hope and light—an example of what is possible in public education even with limited funding but a clear mission and high quality teachers. We do not compete in our school district, we cooperate and share. We learn from our mistakes and share them, too. We do not siphon off money, we collaborate with other schools to solve educational problems.

We have taken seriously a responsibility to build the profession through helping young teachers in training. Our innovative relationship with Quinnipiac University brings into our school multiple teacher-residents, who spend a full year working "side by side" with veteran teachers. Together they build a knowledge base of working in a diverse, urban setting, which can be built upon when those young teacher candidates move on to other schools.

But these are not the goals of many of the new "charter school management organizations." They seek to build more and more charter schools whenever and wherever they can; to profit from these corporate enterprises; to pay high salaries to their management teams. This corporatization of public schooling has understandably brought many people to question the charter school movement—whose trajectory appears now to be more about money than kids.

During the confirmation of Cabinet members in the Trump administration, the Northeast Charter Schools Network to which our stand-alone charter pays dues, endorsed without our knowledge the nomination of Betsy DeVos for Secretary of Education. I was appalled, if not surprised. This endorsement was blatantly self-serving. The only reason that this advocacy group could possibly back Ms. DeVos is because of her open support of large charter school organizations and the corporatization of public education. The fact that Ms. DeVos, when questioned by the Senate panel, did not know the difference between growth and proficiency models, or that the Individuals with Disabilities Education Act was federally legislated, made no apparent difference to the Northeast Charter Schools Network.

So, aside from requesting that my board of directors act to remove our school from the network, I am appealing to those who initiated the charter school movement to stand up for the way this movement began, and to fight against the trajectory it has taken. Not all charter schools are the same—many are small havens of high level teaching, laboratories of good practice that the teaching profession can learn from; classrooms where kids who may not thrive in traditional public schools can flourish. But most important, these small havens are places that, unencumbered by larger district mandates, can provide opportunities to learn and grow the profession; not fill the pockets and egos of those who would build an empire.[3]

"A fanatic," as Winston Churchill once said, "is someone who can't change their mind and can't change the subject." Free-market enthusiasts tend to be fanatical in their defense of the economic theory behind "choice." The arguments used to defend the profit-taking[4] seen at major charter school corporations declare those profits as a CEO's right to profit from the risk they took in a "free market."

No matter how the public perceives these transactions, the defenders of the current charter status quo insist that they are running schools like a free-market business.

The truth is *that they are running things like a business*.

The question is, "What type of business?"

As our experiences with deregulated markets painfully taught us during our last financial market meltdown, deregulation is not a panacea. Commerce without morality may be legal, but the fiscal results are anything but sound. A market with a 43.5 percent failure rate, with 19 percent of those closures (eighty-two sites) occurring *during the school year*, indicates that this contracted service is not being delivered in a fiscally sound or reliable manner.

The current structure of this "free market" in charter schools and vouchers is neither free nor open. What has devolved is a far cry from the idealized free market described and sold to the early adopters at the dawn of the charter school movement. While the data confirms that 23 percent of charter holders *do not need to be regulated to do the right thing*, it also points to 77 percent of charter holders needing a tighter set of what Milton Friedman referred to as "the rules of the game" to guide their financial practices.

As charter growth continues, it is time to rethink the realities of the economic model guiding our charter laws. We have over twenty-seven years of experience with this model. That experience should be guiding our need to change and improve the model.

It isn't. We have lost our local voice in the political processes governing our commitments to educate our children.

NOTES

1. The initiative to hold a "future search" in the district was directed by the author, who was a building-level principal at the time. Over 180 citizens chosen by their selectmen for their diverse political views were invited to participate in this event over several days. The initiative was community-driven, with representation from the state level present.

2. The Monadnock Regional School Board also had visionary leadership on its board. At great political cost, this board and the board chair backed the district's chartering efforts.

3. Anne Dichele, PhD, is board chair of the Side By Side Charter School in Norwalk, Connecticut, and a professor at the Quinnipiac University School of Education.

4. Advocates of this model insist that making a profit is a primary requirement of the charter marketplace. This is referred to as a "profit motive." This correlates with Friedman's oft-stated belief that the only social purpose of a business is to make a profit for its shareholders.

Chapter Nine

"All Politics Is Local"

In the previous chapter, the words of Anne Dichele were presented. Anne is the type of educator who believes in a locally connected charter school model. "Side by Side" in the name of her school speaks volumes about her organization's commitment to work with the local public schools.

Liberals and conservatives once agreed about the importance of local control and local politics. Tip O'Neill and Ronald Reagan both understood the importance of local government and local political issues and their importance to the health of our democracy.

The majority of charter laws, as currently written, are the antithesis of local control driven by local politics at the grassroots level. The "need" for new charter school laws has always been initiated at the state or federal level, not locally. This should have marked this issue as a political red herring.

We ignored our own historical experiences with privatization while devising the current model. As a nation, we have tried private education models based on economics before. Doing the same thing over and over and expecting different results is the definition of insanity. Privatizing public education has been tried many times.

A purely market-driven model that relied on parents paying for their own children's education was the only educational path available prior to the Civil War.

Individual states had a version of pay-for-your-child's-education when there weren't any publicly funded schools available in those states. As will be demonstrated, this pay-for-your-child's-education model represents the "good old days" to which privatizers ultimately want to return. Those days weren't so good.

The current tax-subsidized model is a temporary fix on the road to full privatization, where parents pay for their children's education. Proponents of this goal use the phrase "Starving the beast of public education" to describe their diversion of public funds to private profit-driven enterprises. Advocates for this version of "public" education in a democratic republic have confused the goals of a capitalistic economic model—profits—with the goals of a democratic republic—liberty and justice for all.

Local choice in communities *led those communities* to build the first publicly sponsored schools in this republic. These were the traditional one-room schoolhouses that mixed all ages together in one room. The resulting system of a free and appropriate education for all children in our republic did not come into play nationally until 1918. This was the year when compulsory education laws were passed at the national level. Significantly, this was the same decade when child labor laws were enacted (1919).

The 1991 Minnesota State Legislature's passage of charter school laws[1] marked the beginning phase of an actualized charter school movement in the United States. That charter movement now encompasses forty-three states and the District of Columbia. The latest state to enact charter school laws is Kentucky (2017). The economic theory defining the use of free-market economics to provide voucher payments and charters paid for with public funds dates to the middle of the twentieth century.

The first public charter school was developed and established in Minnesota in 1992. In an August 31, 2012, discussion on National Public Radio, commentator and former educator Claudio Sanchez noted that "City Academy in St. Paul, Minnesota, became the nation's first publicly funded, privately run charter school when it opened its doors in 1992. Its founders, *all veteran public school teachers*, had tried but failed to create new programs for struggling students in their own schools. The school helped launch a movement that has since grown to 5,600 (2012 number) charter schools across the U.S. But back in the late 1980s, it faced strong resistance."

The figures at the end of 2017 from the National Alliance for Public Charter Schools indicate that "in 2016–2017, there are more than 6,900 charter schools, enrolling an estimated 3.1 million students. Over the past 10 years, enrollment in charter schools has nearly tripled—from 1.2 million students in 2006–2007 to an estimated 3.1 million in 2016–2017. Between 2015–2016 and 2016–2017 estimated charter school enrollment has increased by over 200,000 students. The estimated 7 percent growth in charter school enrollment between fall 2015 and fall 2016 demonstrates continued parental demand for high-quality educational options."

When given the option of choosing their child's school, super moms and dads chose what they believed were super schools.[2] The facts indicate that most of the high-performing charters are locating in school districts and neighborhoods *that are already academically excelling*. That is, they typically have "A"-rated schools to begin with.

Superman, it seems, is not locating where his services are needed most. When he does, those charters are the most likely to flounder financially. As any businessperson knows, the key to real estate success is based on three things: "location, location, and location."

The efforts by state legislatures, the federal government, and charter advocacy groups (funded largely by corporate foundations) to promote what is referred to as "school choice" are described in the literature with language that is designed to make this economic theory of action appear to be a conservative, democratic ideal. The financial reality is that the model that has evolved is neither fiscally conservative nor democratic.

Words such as *parental choice, freedom to choose, competition*, and *innovation* are designed to lull the public into thinking that "educational choices" are something to which they, as free individuals in a republic, are *entitled*. A consumer "choice" model has fostered the mindset that we have the "right" to pick any type of education that we, as individuals, choose.

Choice was a right we had prior to charter and voucher legislation.

Consumer choice prior to 1991 meant that the consumer also had the responsibility to pay for this freely made choice. The newly gained "right to choose" is a right that charter advocates insist they provided to the public. That right is now paid for by taxes on all of the chooser's fellow citizens. An entitlement mentality is encouraged in this redefining of the meaning and purpose of mandatory education laws.

An entitlement mentality should be the antithesis of a capitalist-based economic theory's mindset.

The first mandatory-attendance public school laws were set up to provide common schools that prepared a child for life as a citizen of a democratic republic. They were not set up to isolate our children in self-selected educational silos administered and directed by contracted businesses. If that is what we wanted as consumers, we had the right to opt out by attending a school that we, the consumer, paid for.

Common schools were not set up to make money. They were set up to deliver public education in an economical, locally controlled manner. Consider the example of publicly financed parks.

We have a right to use publicly funded parks. We do not have a right to take our share of the funds used for this purpose and apply it to our privately-owned country club's membership fees. A contracted maintenance company servicing the park properties does not own the park's real estate and equipment. Our community owns this asset. We also have a right to tax-funded police and fire protection. We can't take our share of those services' revenue sources and pay for a security company to oversee our property as a free-market "choice."

The funds for contractual agreements with charter corporations are taxpayer funds from the state and federal governments. The school-choice economic model redefines those funds as "payments to a contractor" for a contracted service. A transaction sending publicly sourced money into private hands is used to justify the lack of financial oversight that follows.

The stated theory is that once the money is in the contractor's possession, "they have more freedom over their budgets, staffing, curricula, and other operations." In practice, this means that there is scant financial oversight regarding how voucher and charter school revenues are used once the contractor receives the money.

We are told that is how "free-market" government service contracts work. The economic model used to defend charters' financial freedom to spend contracted funding as they please is an anomaly. Most government-contracted services include bidding and *guarantees of product delivery*. The behavior of the contractor is regulated by the contract's terms. This type of oversight requires little if any legislative change. It does require regulation.

NOTES

1. Minnesota's state charter laws are ranked sixteenth in the latest ranking by the pro-charter Center for Educational Reform. The state was ranked third by the National Alliance for Charter Schools, another pro-charter advocacy group, in 2017. The difference in ranking can be attributed to different opinions about how Minnesota's state charter laws are viewed by the "Choice Friendliness" rating agencies.

2. The implication in *Waiting for Superman*, a pro-privatization film, is that charter owners are the supermen of public school choice, saving children from "failing public schools."

Chapter Ten

Deregulating a Public Good

You can't legislate morality.

—Barry Goldwater

No, but you can regulate behavior.

—Martin Luther King Jr.

Capitalistic marketplaces for consumer services, the idealized free market described in Dr. Friedman's economic theory, *are behaving exactly* like they behaved during the last financial meltdown. As a result of this unregulated behavior, the majority of charter sites (82 percent) have become overleveraged with property and assets that are under water.

We have seen this type of financial behavior in a deregulated market before.

Meltdowns that described the failed deregulated junk bond markets in the last century, the savings and loan scandals, pension fund heists, and corporate hostile takeovers, fit a pattern of corporate behavior in an unregulated free market.

CEOS of charter companies are behaving exactly like CEOs did prior to the last financial meltdown. They are looking out for themselves. Business decisions and profit motives trump educational decisions in this model when it is applied to an educational marketplace.

All of this is done legally because the charter laws legalized this definition of charter-contracted services by deregulating school financial rules. In the last market meltdown, CEOs still, to the outrage of the general public, collected their bonuses and options.

Are we really surprised that it is going on in this new "free market"?

When we rely on humans to self-regulate their financial behavior without a set of socially acceptable norms guiding them, we have created a marketplace with no real "rules of the game."[1] Self-regulation of behavior is something that we struggle with constantly. It is no surprise that the data indicates that only 23 percent of the charter marketplace is behaving in a socially responsible way with the money it is given to educate our children.

Attitudes and intentions guide our personal behaviors. Laws and regulations are guidelines for our behaviors in a democratic society.

Without laws and regulations, we rely on an individual's self-regulation to guide an individual actor's behavior in a free market. While fighting the monopolistic trusts of his time, Teddy Roosevelt spoke about one of the key components that needed to be in an American education: "To educate a man and to not teach him manners is tantamount to raising a menace to society." Manners are agreed-upon ways we behave toward one another.

Regulations codify expected behaviors.

There was a reason why Moses needed the Ten Commandments.

During the civil rights era, Barry Goldwater insisted that "you cannot legislate morality," to which Dr. Martin Luther King Jr. responded, "No, but you can regulate behavior." Charter laws legislated an economic theory of action and applied that economic model to a public good. Regulation is needed to regulate the financial behaviors seen in the data from twenty-five years of deregulated charter contracting.

The current charter laws are clear. Charters are businesses operating in a free market, and as such, their only social responsibility is to make a profit, provided that they provide the contracted service.

So, who is minding the store?

NOTE

1. Dr. Friedman referred to the need for rules of the game as a vital part of free markets. The current system has no real equivalent to a set of "Ten Commandments" regarding financial behavior in this marketplace.

Chapter Eleven

The Myth of Self-Correcting Free Markets

We are told that the regulating factor in charter contracts is academic performance and consumer demand for educational choices. The second part of the definition of charter schools states, "In exchange for 'freedom' from regulations, charters must deliver academic results and there must be enough community demand for them to remain open."

The guiding premise in this statement is that a "free market" will pick financial winners and losers based on the academic performances at those schools.

The model predicts that parents will choose to exit academically failing schools, taking the educational funding associated with their child with them. Community demand for charter providers is theorized to come from parental demand for academic performance. An espoused "exit theory" will regulate financial success.

Simply stated, it goes like this: Parents are making "informed" consumer choices based on academic performance; therefore, academic data results will lead parents to vote with their feet. The Grand Canyon Institute, a nonpartisan think tank at Arizona State University, tested that theory's basic premise. *GCI found that there is no correlation between a charter's academic rating and its financial performance ratings.*

During fiscal year 2018, the academic "A through F" scores in Arizona *excluded* 35 percent of the charter choices in the state. These "choices," mostly online schools, received a Not Rated (NR) academic scoring. To be clear, this NR status was the result of approximately one-third of all charter contractors *opting to become listed as "Alternative Schools" when the academic ranking scores became a method to determine the cut points for academic closures by the charter board in 2014.*

Those contractors purposely lowered their academic bar to an alternative status.[1] *According to the theory, parents should have left these academic underachievers as they lowered their academic standards. They didn't.*

The exit theory espoused by choice advocates is not validated in the data. The theories and research regarding why people exit, use their voice to change an organization, or remain loyal to an organization are clear (Hirschman, 1970). People choose schools and communities in which to live for different reasons.

Academics are not the only reason people choose a school. This is not to say that academic choice does not exist or that it is not correlated at all with *some parents'* choices. There is *some* parental choice that is driven by academic excellence decisions. However, there are many other factors motivating "consumers of educational services" to exit their public or charter schools.

We would not have to establish player eligibility rules for sports if all parents were choosing based solely on academics. Online schools with horrendous dropout rates (49 percent) and NR ratings are not being chosen because of their stellar academics. *They are being chosen for convenience or as a last resort.*

People choosing a Catholic school education when charters did not exist, like the parents of the author, were choosing based on a religious choice—a religious educational choice they paid for.[2] Protestants and other religiously affiliated parents choosing diocesan parochial schools did so because of a perceived notion that discipline at those parochial schools was better than at their local public school. Incidentally, there were agnostics and atheists present at the Catholic schools the author attended.

The financial decision made by the diocesan hierarchy to allow non-Catholics to attend the school was just that—financial. Non-Catholics pay more for tuition to this day. Parish-level scholarships to Catholic schools are only available to parish members.

The data regarding who is controlling certain sectors of the voucher and tax credit scholarship market and how *those donated funds are allocated is clearly religious in nature.* As an example, the AZ Christian Scholarship Fund, Catholic Scholarship Funds, and fifty-five other "sanctioned" scholarship fund-collecting agencies in Arizona are, by and large, religious placements. *Fully 55 percent of all tax credit scholarships are used at religious schools.*

The charter laws also allow charter holders who are declared practicing pastors, bishops, and clergy (including imams, priests, nuns, and rabbis) of the local denominations to hold charter contracts. These charter holders' positions in the community as religious leaders often become the "reason" for the parental choice, *not academics.*

This observation is based on experience in this market and comments made by parents regarding their religious leaders preaching which charter or private scholarship-funded school to send their children to at their services.[3]

Who has created this implied "consumer demand" for choice? Hint: It wasn't the parents.

When asked to rate three things—their child's public school, local public schools, and the nation's public schools—*parents gave an A or B to their children's local public school 77 percent of the time.* The general public gave their local public schools an A or B rating 49 percent of the time. In contrast, the nation's schools were given an 18 percent rating of either A or B.

The data represents the 2010 ratings[4] of the public's opinion regarding public schools. Clearly most parents were satisfied *with their children's public school* but had a poor opinion of other communities' public schools and a dismal opinion of the nation's schools. Those opinions were influenced by the war on America's public schools, a purposeful assault on public education (Bracey, 2002; Bracey, 2003).

Who is choosing, and what are we losing when parents take a government subsidy to opt out of our community schools?

Language about public district schools put out by the organizations lobbying for charter schools and vouchers describes public school districts as "immune to change, government schools," while they call districts "bureaucracies."[5] One choice advocacy group lists multiple states *with* charter school laws on the books as "moribund" because those legislatures have decided to put in reasonable growth and financial restrictions on the charter markets in their states.

The rating system used is an economic "freedom of choice" ranking at these organizations, not an academic achievement ranking. This is evident when the charter law ratings are compared to the state's academic ratings.

The list of states that *are* high-performing academically by national academic standards is virtually *the inverse* of those states with high rankings for their charter laws from charter advocacy groups. Vermont receives a 55 percent from the charter advocacy group Ed Reform and an 81 percent on their academic ratings from Quality Counts,[6] a national assessment of school quality put out yearly by *Education Week*. Massachusetts is ranked at 68 percent for its charter law friendliness scores by Ed Reform and at 86.5 percent academically (first place) in Quality Counts.

There *is no correlation between the state's charter law friendliness scores and academic performance ratings. When placed side by side (Charter Friendliness scores and Academic Rankings by state) the lists' scores do not correlate. Likewise, the academic grades of charters are not predictors of a charter company's financial viability.*

The connection of capitalism, privatization, choice, and academic quality was first postulated by Milton Friedman. When Dr. Friedman was comparing public school systems to his economic theory's solution set of vouchers and privately held charters, he chose to praise the "free-market" economic model of the private schools of the 1960s:

> Every private school must satisfy its customers—parents paying tuition and benefactors who contribute funds to the school. Every private school now pays its teachers according to their merit. If it did not, its "better" teachers would be hired away by its competitors and it would be left with the poorer ones. Its customers would sooner or later discover what is happening and desert it.[7]

Friedman followed this glowing free-market picture of private education with his oft-repeated thoughts on the public school system, the "government competition" to private schools at the time. As he wrote in *Newsweek* on December 5, 1983:

> The situation is wholly different with a *socialist enterprise* like the public school system, or, for that matter, a private monopoly.[8] The true customers of the public schools—parents and children—have come to exercise less and less influence over the schools as the schools have become more and more centralized and bureaucratic. When school districts were numerous and small, parents could exercise considerable influence. A superintendent or principal who misjudged the "merit" of teachers—in the eyes of consumers—would not have remained in these positions for long.

From the 1980s through today, most public schools have shifted to site-based management and budget building. This was an innovative management move by public schools to put economic and decision-making power regarding curriculum at the local level.

With ten charter companies controlling three-fourths of new charter enrollments at companies that are managed and controlled by Educational Management Groups, isn't it fair to ask whether site-based management is compromised at charter-contracted school sites run by mega-charter organizations?

A rethinking of Friedman's statement, "The situation is wholly different with a socialist enterprise like the public school system, or, for that matter, a private monopoly," is in order.

Monopoly and oligarchies are becoming the name of the charter game.

What does the financial audit data on net losses and net gains tell us about the efficacy of this economic model?

NOTES

1. The academic reporting at the charter board for FY 2012 through 2014 clearly shows this change of status. Every charter was evaluated by reviewing the data provided at the ASBCS website.

2. At the time, those payments for Catholic school tuition were not tax-deductible. In Arizona, "choice scholarships" provide parents and businesses with a tax credit.

3. During the anti-Catholic eras of American history, the Catholic Church made it a mortal sin to send one's child to public school if a parish school was available. This guilt-driven option was not a freedom to choose by any stretch of the imagination. The reasons for this edict were the openly anti-Catholic stories in *McGuffey's Reader* and the leadership of the public schools in New York.

4. See *The Public's View on American Schools* from 1985 through 2010. https://news.gallup.com/poll/142658/americans-views-public-schools-far-worse-parents.aspx.

5. In a recent advertisement for reelection, Arizona's Governor Ducey made a point of saying that he did not want more money going to bureaucracies. As of FY 2017, charter schools spend 2 to 1 the amount that districts spend on management. Source: Superintendent's Report for FY 2017.

6. https://www.edweek.org/ew/collections/quality-counts-2018-state-grades/index.html.

7. At the time, private schools did pay better than public schools. Today, private schools typically pay far less than public schools, and charters pay their teachers less than public schools while providing fewer benefits.

8. It will be shown that 78 percent of all new charter student growth during the last four years in Arizona has gone to ten large charter groups. These ten are privately held companies with an oligarchical lock on those schools.

Chapter Twelve

Financial "Tells"

The failure rates at charters and newly minted private schools since 1991 are telling us something about this free-market model. There are other tells in the data that should be alerting state legislators and the public. In gambling parlance, the house is losing too much, a sign that the game is rigged in favor of the players. Someone is cheating.

Who is choosing, and who is losing?

The net gain on the year for all charters in this analysis was under 2 percent. A poor *overall* ROI (Return on Investment) for an industry with revenues that exceeded $1.5 billion at the 564 sites assessed. Are all charters barely squeaking by? No.

The figures on "Net Gains" *of the top ten companies in this group showed they had captured $28 million (52 percent) of the net gains at charters in FY 2017. These companies were financial juggernauts in this marketplace. In business terms, the charter market is consolidating.*

One would expect, based on those companies' stellar financial performances, that these firms would also be highly rated on academic performances. Not really. In fact, only two of those ten companies have "A" and "B" ratings at their sites.

Six charter groups in the top ten financial winners are rated "C." The two online schools in the list are "Not Rated"; both have dropout rates greater than 20 percent; one has a 49 percent dropout rate. Clearly academic prowess and economic success are not related.

What about the corporate designation? Five of the companies in the group are registered as for-profit corporations; five are listed as nonprofits.

Only one of the firms among these market share and financially successful winners provides its employees with access to the state retirement system. Two provide state retirement benefits for management only (these employees

Table 12.1. Fiscal 2017 Net Losses and Gains Analysis for 264 Arizona Charter Sites

Net Losses at 221 Sites with Net Losses	$(–34,838,210)
Net Gains of 243 Sites with Profits, i.e., Net Gains	$52,169,173

Source: Consolidated Net Losses and Net Gains by Charter Holder for FY 2017 from Audits

are not "leased," which allows the company to pay their salaries directly). This "special group of employees" includes the owners. The other seven companies[1] *in the top ten provide a "matching retirement plan" of between 4 and 6 percent.*

The actual level of those "matches" was calculated based on audit reporting on retirement accounts. Statistics comparing the actual amounts contributed show that the contribution rate in 2017 was 2.13 percent. The state retirement system match for a participating charter school group is 11.2 percent. A substantial savings which then can be paid out to the firm controlling the teacher leasing. In all of the cases surveyed, this leasing firm was a related party.

These profit figures do not include profits taken at for-profit subsidiaries of the charter business. Grand Canyon Institute's public policy papers have estimated, using a forensic analysis of the data, that those companies are making between 10 to 15 percent profit on those related party transactions.

This percentage estimate figure is based on an analysis of the outgoing payments to the subsidiary and comparing that to the expense in that category on the audits (a forensic accounting approach was utilized for this analysis).[2] Real estate transactions, refinancing, and distributions are analyzed later in this document, as they relate to the overall profitability of this market sector.

There *are profits to be made in the charter contracting market.* Graph 1 shows that a segment of the market is profiting and another segment is profiteering (defined in our data as having a net profit *per student* greater than or equal to $1,000 net gain per student).

A paradigm shift regarding how we fund and govern public education has occurred. We have moved from an educational theory of action (publicly funded and governed schools) to an economic theory of action (capitalist free-market and private corporation-governed schools), and it has played out over the last twenty-five years (Kuhn, 1962).

The forensic accounting used by the research practitioner performing the studies analyzed the financial results of privatization *rather than the stated intentions of the market theory behind charter schools and voucher laws. Results documented in hard data on both educational market sectors, public and private, were performed. This was done by comparing market sectors.*

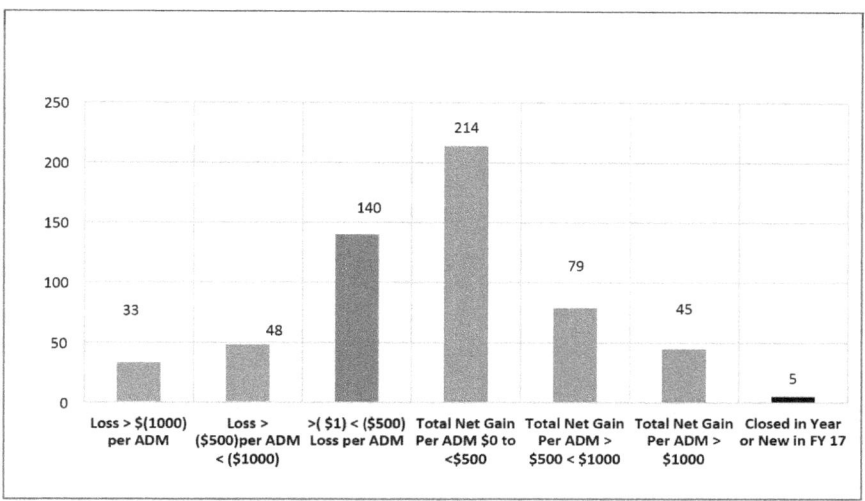

Figure 12.1. FY 2017 Net Losses and Net Gains at Arizona Charter Sites
Source: Net Losses and Net Gains from FY 2017 Divided by the Total ADM at Each Site. Grand Canyon Institute research paper: "Red Flags: Overleveraged Properties," www.grandcanyoninstitute.org

COMPARING MARKET SECTORS' DEBT

In any free-market sector analysis, money talks. Money owed on charter long-term lease-adjusted debt *talks loudly* when *charter contractors in Arizona have a market share of 16 percent of the students and hold $2.6 billion (33 percent) of long-term debt and lease commitments outstanding on all school properties. Charter real estate holdings have a current (FY 2017) depreciated market value of $1.4 billion.* Charter corporations hold only 7 percent of school real estate in the state.

School districts, by contrast, have 84 percent of the students in the state and control ten times the property and assets ($20.7 billion) that charter contractors hold. District long-term debt is currently $5.1 billion (67 percent of all school debt). None of Arizona's districts is under water on its properties. Regulations and policies safeguarding taxpayers from overzealous building projects in a district are validated by that district's debt-to-assets ratio, which was 1 to 4 at the end of FY 2017.

The data on property and debt points to one market sector (districts) that is paying off long-term debt as it accumulates commonly held assets, while the other sector (charters) is continuously refinancing debt and committing to long-term leases on property that the public has no equity stake in. The charter market functions by constantly refinancing its long-term lease-adjusted debt.

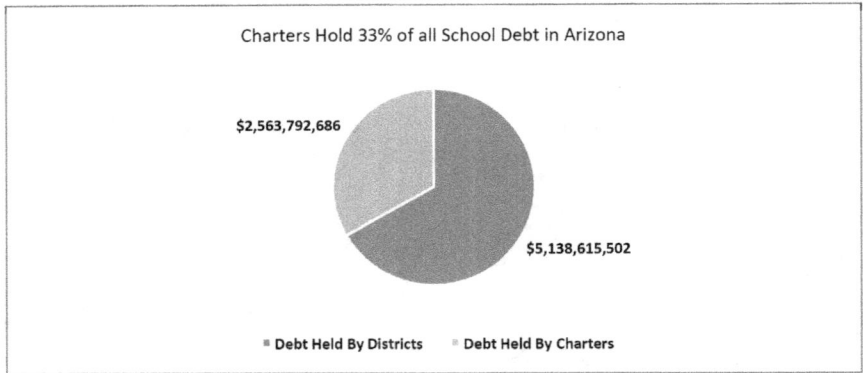

Figure 12.2. FY 2017 Arizona Charter and District Long-Term Lease-Adjusted Debt
Source: Collated Audit Data on Long-Term Lease-Adjusted Debt from FY 2017

It is during these refinancing phases that management takes a profit from the real estate being financed. This financial fact is seen in the ratio of long-term, lease-adjusted debt to property in both market sectors (charter and district). The growth of debt in both sectors is on the same course, with the two-year moving average overlapping the growth curve in districts and charters.

The data reflects twenty-five years of charter activity in this area. The long-term effects of constant refinancing are manifest in the data[3] and in commitments to long-term leases with related parties.

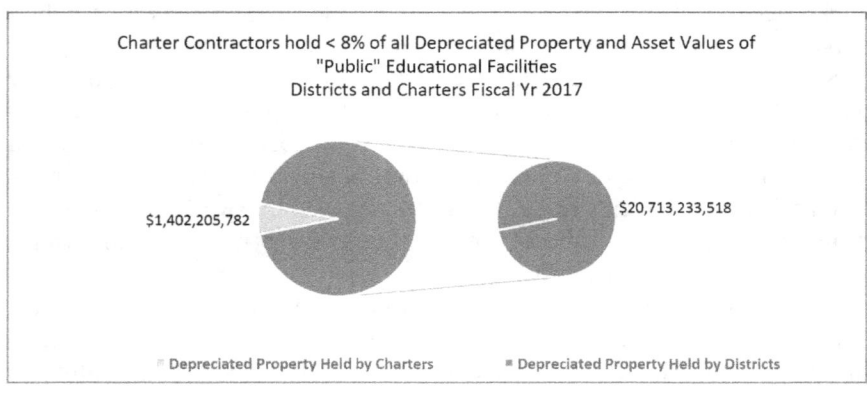

Figure 12.3. FY 2017 AZ Depreciated Value of Educational Properties in This Market Sector
Source: Collated Audit Data on Long-Term Lease-Adjusted Debt from FY 2017

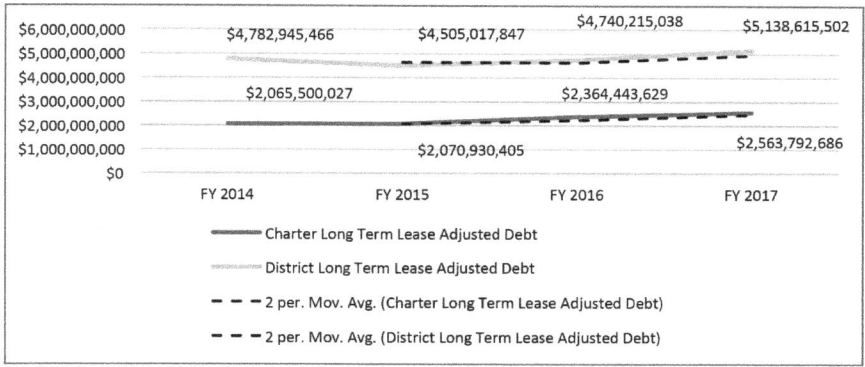

Figure 12.4. Four-Year Trend of Two Market Sectors, Long-Term Lease-Adjusted Debt
Source: Collated Long-Term Debt Adjusted for Leases from Audits and AZDOE Reports from FY 2014 to FY 2017

Simply stated: Districts have a 1 to 4 debt-to-property ratio, while charters have a debt-to-property ratio of 2.6 to 1.4. These figures represent an average, not the worst-case scenario or the best cases in the data. The totals show that charters *as a whole* (82 percent of all sites) are overleveraged and under water on their property and assets.

At the end of FY 2017, 463 (82 percent of 564 under the Arizona State Board for Charter Schools) charter sites were under water on their long-term lease-adjusted debt. The under-water firms were under water by a total of $1,153,517,094. The 101 sites (18 percent of 564) that were not under water had a total positive balance of $8,069,810. Not one district property in Arizona is in this precarious state. The sum of these two offsetting figures is represented by the –$1.6 billion figure.

To be clear, it is *their (the charter holders') property*, not the public's commonly held properties,[4] that are under water. The FY 2017 depreciated value of all charter schools in Arizona was $1,402,205,782. The total long-term lease-adjusted debt (lease commitments) on these properties is *$2,563,792,686.* When we subtract the second figure (the long term lease adjusted debt) from the first figure (the depreciated value of the properties) we arrive at the amount of money that the industry is underwater on its debt.

Arizona's charter market was under water by –$1,161,586,904 at the end of FY 2017, resulting in an unsustainable debt-to-equity ratio of 0.55 to 1 (long-term lease-adjusted debt on the depreciated value[5] of those properties). Only 55 percent of the equity supporting charter bonds is from their property and asset market value. The rest is based on anticipated ADM revenues from backpacks full of cash. The delivery of that revenue depends on *actual* ADM counts.

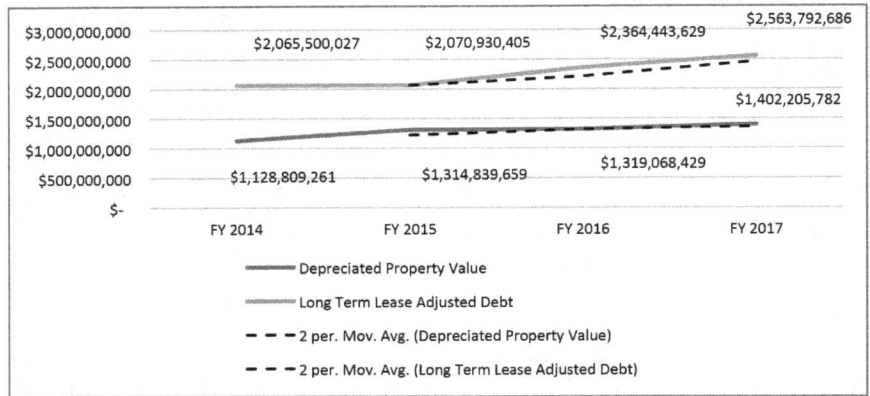

Figure 12.5. Four Years of Depreciated Property to Long-Term Lease Adjusted Debt
Source: Collated Audit Data on Long-Term Lease-Adjusted Debt from FY 2014 to FY 2017

The problem is growing. Preliminary figures on FY 2018 show −$1.5 billion of under-water properties. Four years of ever-increasing debt loads are shown in figure 12.5.

The indebtedness of charters has grown at a much greater rate (more than 2 to 1) than the growth in the property values of all charters from FY 2014 to FY 2017. *These statistics do not include short-term debt or when a charter uses "factoring" to borrow money on its revenue stream.* Lease commitments, which must be paid, are part of the lease-adjusted debt calculations. Only verifiable data, that is, data listed on the audits or on IRS form 990, were used.

Projections of ADM[6] growth *are not being met at 241 out of 427 charter groups as of June 2017.* The charter market's ADM growth is being captured by the top ten charter companies (73 percent of all ADM growth over four years). ADM projections that were used in calculations regarding the feasibility and funding of Educational Revenue Bonds have not kept pace with debt obligations.

A total of 238 of 427 charters lost ADM in Arizona. Statistics in other states mirror this consolidation figure (Society for Economic Anthropology [U.S.] Meeting [2006: Ventura Calif.], Browne, & Milgram). Two hundred thirty-eight charters either lost ADM or had a marginal gain of .5 percent of ADM (thirty-eight charters) between FY 2014 and FY 2017.

Table 12.2 shows that 73 percent of ADM growth between those years went to ten companies. *The top five companies captured 60 percent of ADM gains over four years.* Current 2018 trends are consistent with the four-year trend noted here.

Table 12.2. ASBCS Financial Ratings for 2016–2017, All Sites

Fiscal Year 2016–2017		
Total Sites Evaluated[1]	Meets	Does Not Meet
564	413 73.23%	151 26.77%
72 of these charter sites had prior closures in their corporate history.		
		Red Mark on ASBCS Financials
Sites that were not counted in this dataset 15		77 Sites 13.65%

[1] Reason for not counting the 15 sites: 8 sites were a part of a University program. Four sites were tribal entities and three sites were part of a larger organization that had other real estate holdings in its real estate portfolio.

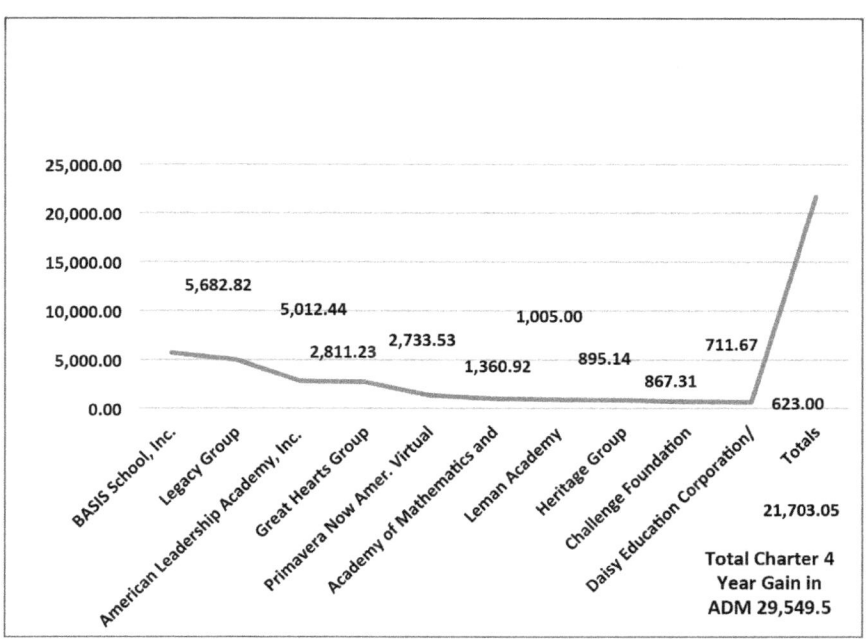

Figure 12.6. New ADM Distribution over Four Years (FY 2014 through FY 2017) Top Ten Companies' Share of Market Growth
Source: Annual Superintendent's Report from FY 2017 ADM, counts adjusted for change in May 2018

The espoused theory of action (i.e., the theory's predictions for how the economic theory will play out) and the theories in use (quantifiable[7] and observable financial effects) are stated and documented in this effort.

The meta-analysis supporting this work was started in 1999,[8] when the author enthusiastically ventured into the charter market for the first time. Those charters, located in New Hampshire, still exist. One is controlled by its local community, the other by the educators managing the school and their boards.

Figure 12.6 shows the distribution of ADM over four years. This is the market reality. The charters that did not make it onto this graph are sharing the remainder of student growth. University charters, which are not under the ASBCS's jurisdiction, gained over two thousand students in this time period. The market is consolidating around ten charter companies *and the state's university charters.*

NOTES

1. Special note on counting: When any researcher counts charters, he or she runs into the issue of how those companies are listed in various counts. The states count each charter as one charter; a single charter can hold multiple sites. A charter corporation may control multiple charters and multiple sites. For example, at the end of FY 2017, there were 233 charter holders in Arizona; they controlled a total of 427 charters and 579 sites. The statistics used in reporting always clarify which number is being used, sites or charters. In fairness to the State Charter Board, our statistics only include the charter sites of which this board has oversight, that is, university charters and other authorizers, municipalities and tribal charters were not used in our analysis.

2. Example of the process: A payment to an employee leasing subsidiary was recorded at $33M. Payroll costs on the same audit revealed a total payroll expenditure of $30.5M. The difference of $2.5M was captured as a profit, after any operational costs, by the employee leasing subsidiary. Teachers who are leased employees are not eligible for any state retirement system benefits. The company "saves" the 11.2 percent contribution rate they would have made to that system by leasing its teachers. The same company offers its own matching plan, which will pay up to 6 percent of the employee's salary into the plan. Evaluation of the rate at which this fund is actually funded revealed that only 1 percent of payroll is being matched. Reason: The employees do not make enough to fund their contribution. See also the Related Party Expenditures figure in the Introduction.

3. See figures 12.2 and 12.3 in this chapter.

4. This fact of ownership effectively removes these private properties from any emergency management uses of those properties. The assets do not belong to the community.

5. Critics of our reports suggest that we did not accommodate for depreciation. We did. Depreciation applies to both market sectors, public and private.

6. ADM is reported by charter, not individual sites. In FY 2017 there were 427 charters held by 239 companies. Those companies had 579 sites. Our dataset did not include the 15 sites that were held by universities, tribal entities, or co-held by larger social service agencies, such as the Boys Club and Chicanos Por la Causa. This was done to avoid counting non-school properties in our equations and to eliminate organizations with other funding sources beyond state and federal educational funding.

7. For example, the data on Arizona Charter Schools gathered by the state for its annual superintendent's reports consistently shows that charters spend, on average, twice what districts do on administrative costs. Source: FY 2014 through FY 2017 State Annual Financial Reviews by Category. Districts also outspend, as a percentage, charters in the classroom expenditure categories. Data regarding this statistic is provided within this book.

8. Prior to receiving the USDOE Grant in FY 2001, the district had initiated efforts to privately create a new school.

Chapter Thirteen

Espoused Theories versus Theories in Use

The economic theory of action behind charter legislation differs significantly from the educational theory of action for chartering public schools put forward by Dr. Budde in 1973. While some of Dr. Budde's original language was maintained by choice advocacy groups, additional language justifying the economic model at the core of today's charter market has been added.

The use of quotation marks around words associated with the marketing of charters is deliberate in this work. An intentional effort has been made in this work to include the original language used in espousing the current version of charter schools. Language has been used by the choice advocacy industry to disguise the fact that an economic theory of action is at the center of this privatization of our "public schools."

This covert and overt use of language, with phrases that appeal to the public's instincts to trust the "free market" to act in a manner that will cause the desired financial effect, insidiously blocks our ability to see what is really going on. That desired effect is stated as "personal choice" for our children's educational services. That ability to "choose" is supposed to provide competition to districts and force public education to "run schools like businesses."[1]

This mental picture of an idealized free-market approach clouds our ability to see what this has really meant in practice. Using corporate raider terms from the 1990s, a well-disguised *hostile financial takeover of public education is occurring*. This is a calculated and deliberate undermining of publicly provided and locally governed education.

Who could argue with the following quote?

> Education is best provided by the free market, achieving greater quality and efficiency with more diversity of choice. Schools should be managed locally to achieve greater accountability and parental involvement. Recognizing that the

education of children is inextricably linked to moral values, we would return authority to parents to determine the education of their children, without interference from government. Parents should have control of all funds expended for their children's education.[2]

This economic theory of action is based on the following premises:

- We, the citizens of the republic, are "consumers of educational services."
- Charters and vouchers allow us, the consumers of this educational service, the "freedom"[3] to choose how we fulfill our needs as consumers in a capitalist free market without direct cost to ourselves.
- The educational service providers contract their services to the state government, which pays them a fee for this service from state and federal tax revenues.

The theory considers tax revenues as payments for contracted educational services, and charter legislation ensures that once that transaction (the transfer of funds) takes place, the owners of the charter are unencumbered by regulations.

They, the educational service providers, are free to spend the money as they see fit to deliver on the contract.

The economic theory predicts that for this contracted service to survive, economically charters or private schools must provide academic results *or the parents will take their children to a different educational contractor*. The restrictions and regulations still apply to the competitor, the local school district, which is just another "choice" in this economic model.

Private and religious schools have the same rules under which they always operated; however, under the new rules, they are recipients of tax-sourced revenues.

Another economic choice has been made by individual citizens. As a result, that public money is no longer available to fund local district schools and charters. It has either been removed from the state's revenue stream through a tax credit or put onto a voucher debit card issued to an individual consumer of educational services.

CONSUMER CHOICE WITHOUT CONSUMER RESPONSIBILITY FOR THAT CHOICE

It is the underlying "free-market" theory articulated in the rest of the Libertarian political party's educational platform being cited in this chapter that most Americans espousing "freedom of choice" would find troubling. The rest of this educational platform does not reflect our traditional views on what is meant by a "free and appropriate public education" for America's children.

The platforms specifically call for the end of all government support for public education.[4]

The words used implicitly question the meaning of the Constitution's use of the term *general welfare* and the ability of any level of government to collect taxes for that purpose. This turn of phrase is deliberate.

This interpretation of the government's power to raise taxes for the common welfare was debated early on in the republic's history. There is a reason the country took until 1919 to declare the need for universal common schools.

We have the founders' response, which they gave in one of the Federalist Papers. We do not have to guess at the founders' intent regarding the government's right to levy taxes for our common defense and for the general welfare of the society.

The justification for the government's ability to tax for the public good rests, as will be demonstrated, on the US Constitution's use of the term *general welfare*, sometimes referred to as "the common good." The founders were clear about their support of this definition.

Schooling alone, like Robert Putnam's *Bowling Alone*, takes a hard look at the loss of political and social capital in a republic when we choose to send our children to different schools from the ones that their neighbors attend.

Our responsibilities to our community and to one another have been transferred by state legislative action to contracted service providers that we, as individuals, have chosen. In states with charter schools, upwards of 16 to 19 percent of our citizens have chosen to school alone rather than at their community-provided schools. Nationally the figure is around 10 percent.

When states legislated rules allowing the financial support from taxes (backpacks full of cash) to follow those children to a privately held charter business, they *intentionally* undercut the local political control of public education. Lost community social capital is tied to that loss of local political capital. There is also *lost economic capital in the community.*

Tax dollars for educating our students that once were spent in town, or at least in the state, are now going out of town, out of state, and out of the country.[5] Microeconomics identifies this type of monetary loss as a capital loss to the local economy, as tax-generated funding is spent outside of the community.

The disdain for any public support, including the use of tax revenues, for educating American children in the Libertarian and mainstream political platforms cited is a *clear and present danger* to the general welfare. As previously examined, John Dewey said, "narrow and unlovely: acted upon, it destroys our democracy." That "clear and present" danger referred to earlier is articulated in another part of the 2008 Libertarian platform and is provided here as a direct quote:

> *Education is best provided by the free market, achieving greater quality and efficiency with more diversity of choice. Schools should be managed locally to achieve greater accountability and parental involvement. Recognizing that the education of children is inextricably linked to moral values we would return authority to parents to determine the education of their children, without interference from government. Parents should have control of all funds expended for their children's education.*

Sounds pretty innocuous. This *updated version* of the party's platform replaced the earlier Libertarian 2000 educational platform. The change was made in order to make the 2008 version palatable to the general public. The original intent is clear in the 2000 version:

> *We advocate the complete separation of education and State. Government schools lead to the indoctrination of children and interfere with the free choice of individuals. Government ownership, operation, regulation, and subsidy of schools and colleges should be ended. We call for the repeal of the guarantees of tax-funded, government-provided education, which are found in most state constitutions.*

Today's Libertarian Party contends that the scope and powers of government should be constrained so as to allow each individual as much freedom of action as is consistent with a like freedom for everyone else: "Thus, they believe that individuals should be free to behave and to dispose of *their property* as they see fit, provided that their actions do not infringe on the equal freedom of others."[6]

The definition of what constitutes "their property" was extended by Milton Friedman's "neighborhood effect," justifying tax revenues following students to their school of choice. The premise of the argument is that the money represented by tax dollars from all citizens now *belongs to the individual to consume educational services as they see fit.*

The money *following the student* is termed "backpacks full of cash" in the literature. This is a belief system that is premised on an individual parent's *entitlement* to public funds for his or her individual consumer choice. Therein lies the "free market" theory problem. The theory counts on taxpayer funding to work. Those taxpayers lose *their choice* regarding where *their money* is going.[7]

This interpretation of "individual freedom" has also led to a privatization of charters' property and assets in most of the states with charter and voucher legislation. The new owners of what were once deemed to be public properties are free to leverage their private property for long-term debt (bonds) and committed long-term leases.[8]

Additional state and federal tax funding is lost when the bondholders are granted tax-free status on those educational revenue bonds, and therefore it is no longer available to support the state's educational obligations.

"Our schools," once the centerpieces of our community life, have become the "my school's assets" of the privatizers. This corporate takeover of formerly public properties has been aided and abetted by state legislatures and federal largesse to charter schools.

Teachers have been turned into corporate employees in this equation. One indicator of what that has meant for those employees is how their benefits have been curtailed. A retirement heist is in progress.

NOTES

1. The phrase, "We are running schools like a business" is commonly used by charter owners and their supporters when defending their financial practices when the public questions some of those practices. Another common phrase is, "Stop thinking like a district."

2. National platform adopted at Denver during the Libertarian Party Convention, May 30, 2008.

3. Thomas Jefferson clearly identified the difference between "freedom" and "liberty." *Freedom* in his writings means to be free from something (i.e., British control). *Liberty* in Jeffersonian writings means to be free to do something. Using the definition of freedom as described could be seen as a call to be "free" from the control of a community's public schools. We will show that this is a false freedom, as the substituted controller at a charter is often an oligarchy. Corporate control still means someone is in control. Your freedom is considered your freedom to leave and choose another provider in this case. The literature on Exit, Voice, and Loyalty contradicts this logic regarding how people make choices.

4. In his 1980 *Free to Choose*, Milton Friedman alluded to educational progress from his voucher and charter solution set leading to a less stratified distribution of wealth. This new thriving middle class would eventually be able to afford to pay for their own children's education. In reality, wealth distribution in the United States has become more concentrated, not less, since 1995 (Friedman, 1980).

5. The laws allow for out-of-state charter educational management firms to manage educational services by setting up charters in states where the contractor has been licensed to operate by the charter authorizers in that state. There are at least nine countries receiving parts of the contractual funds paid to charters in the United States. We do not include normal expenditures for curriculum materials and supplies in this statement. It is a statement regarding salaries, building contracts, and capital expenses. Example: The Gulan Schools throughout the United States, operated from a site in the Poconos in Pennsylvania, are the largest user of federal work visas, as

they import teachers from the Middle East and Europe to work in their schools. This is all legal in the world of contracted educational services, since they provide schools that typically are graded as A or B schools.

6. Quoted from *Encyclopedia Britannica* article by David Boaz: https://www.britannica.com/topic/libertarianism-politics. In this case, their property is being defined as an entitlement to funding that normally would flow to a district educating their children.

7. A counterargument by the charter industry is that we elected our state representatives and they made the rules. This argument does not consider or makes light of the fact that direct local control has been bypassed.

8. The actual wording of the sections of charter law spelling this out in Arizona will be provided.

Chapter Fourteen

Retirement Heist

Private school owners rightfully express their opinion that the teachers they subcontract with for educational services are *their employees.*[1] Taken to the extreme, corporate mindsets regarding employees lead to charter companies and their subsidiaries using related party employment firms to lease their employees (read as teachers, aides, and principals) back to the charter school.

This employee leasing arrangement immediately makes those employees ineligible to participate in the state retirement systems (i.e., they are no longer considered "state" employees since they are "leased" from a related educational management service). One need only imagine the application of this market solution to other public enterprises such as the military or police and fire services.

Ironically, the same state charter legislation often has clauses specifying that charter teachers *are state employees and as such are eligible for the state retirement system.* The new reality is a state retirement system participation rate of 37 percent at charter schools, with another 20 percent of these private companies providing "retirement programs" that have an average *participation rate* of 1 percent of the entire payroll. The match rate the company states they will provide for these optional plans ranges from 4 to 6 percent.

The low participation rate reflects the inability of staff to fund their half of the match rate.[2] In another 43 percent of privately held charters, the companies offer *no retirement or pension option at all to their employees.*[3] This non-participation rate poses a direct threat not only to the long-term financial well-being of these privately employed charter schoolteachers, *but also to the financial health of state retirement systems.*

A new retirement heist[4] is underway, with charter firms collecting "service fees" at their employee leasing firms for leasing teachers *back to their own subsidiary charter schools* (typically 10 to 15 percent of total payroll costs).

Teachers are subcontracted employees in this market variation on acceptable employment practices. They are kept from collecting unemployment during the summer by the charter's use of "intents to hire,"[5] a substitute work guarantee replacing a real teacher's contract like the one that district teachers receive.

This is only one facet of the "leasing of employees" and real estate profiteering going on in this "free-market" sector. Running schools like businesses according to a free-market theory means that "the only social responsibility of a business is to make a profit for its shareholders." The shareholders are typically the charter holders and their corporate boards.

Leasing your teachers is profitable for the corporation.

Management takes a different tack when it comes to their own benefits. Some employees, it appears, are "more equal" than others (Orwell, 1971).

A troubling fact in the data is the oversized salaries of CEOs *who keep themselves in the state retirement system while denying the same benefit to their teachers*. This patently unfair labor practice is done by paying upper management directly from the company's funds rather than through the subsidiary employment firm that "hires" and leases the teachers back to the school.

This means that management's retirement payments from the state will also be oversized, as the average of the last five years of "service" and the length of time in the system determine how much one receives in retirement. Another disturbing trend in the data showed two companies that dropped the retirement system once the charter holder and his or her spouse hit the maximum benefit level.

An equally insidious method used to shortchange employees is seen in several charters with multiple charters and sites. One charter in the group participates in the AZRS and the others have no pension plan at all. It is not hard to guess which one the CEO owner was being paid out of. These practices go unchallenged in a "right to work" state.

Groups that participate in and then drop the retirement system are a drag on the system's financial resources. At the very least, these are what used to be called "unfair labor practices."

At the end of fiscal year 2017, only 36.89 percent of all charter sites participated in the AZ retirement system at all. This percentage includes those that only offer it to their upper management (at least twenty-five sites). Another 31.1 percent of charter schools had some form of retirement match. The actual contribution rate to the match averaged 1 percent of payroll.

A full 32.01 percent *had no retirement benefit* of any kind in their benefit packages.

In fact, charter teachers *never really were state employees*, that is, if the logic of contracted educational services is pursued. These contractors, after all, are private businesses.

State laws allowing this designation as state employees contradict the premise that the state is using tax resources for a private contractor to provide educational services. States do not allow road contractors or other contracted state service companies and their employees to participate in the state retirement system.

A legislative intent, to provide teachers in charters with access to the retirement system, has been sidestepped by charter owners who are intent on maximizing their profits and benefits while profiteering from privately held real estate acquisitions.

NOTES

1. This fact was driven home during a conversation with the first chair of the Arizona Charter School Board. The author was arguing for an increase in wages for the teachers at his schools. The reply was, "They should be happy that I gave them a job." This statement was made to clarify who the teachers were really working for.

2. In Arizona, charter teachers' average pay is 84 percent that of district-employed teachers. Larger gaps are seen at the building administrator level. Gross overpayment of upper management and ownership, along with examples of owners taking either no or little compensation, are all part of the dataset. As noted, 23 percent of the owners are trying to do the right thing with their charter schools. These firms in the 23 percent typically are in the retirement system and fairly compensate their teachers.

3. Source: audit data on pension spending from FY 2014–2017.

4. See *Retirement Heist* by Ellen Schultz (2011).

5. The "intent to hire" is designed so that the employee cannot apply for unemployment during the periods the school is out of session. It is not a guarantee of employment in a "right to work" state.

Chapter Fifteen

Investing in the General Welfare

The capital investors in this marketplace solution's bond markets are typically the same firms that pushed in the past for deregulation of the financial industry, banks, stock indexing, and the now-defunct savings and loan businesses in this country. These financial "investors" hold the outsized debt on charter contractors' assets. The bonds are referred to as "educational revenue bonds," an indication that student counts and the educational revenue from the state are the real backing for the bond.

This arrangement is sold as letting others take the financial risks involved in constructing public schools. We are led to believe that the risk-taker is the charter holder. Not really.

We cite H. L. Mencken: "Nobody ever went broke underestimating the intelligence of the American public."

Tax-free bonds financed by junk bond markets will be shown to be the primary source used by charter school contractors funding their ever-increasing long-term debt. The public is being played for fools once again by the junk bond markets and by Wall Street.

Is this use of taxpayer resources promoting the general welfare or corporate welfare?

The Libertarian, and increasingly the Republican, interpretation of the government's ability to tax for the general welfare, and their political platform advocating the complete separation of education from the government, is a clear and present danger to our democracy. They are two sides of the same political coin.

The question of the government's authority to tax for the general welfare was settled by the founders and resettled by the Civil War.

For a quarter of a century, this twentieth-century political and economic theory of action has been acted upon and applied to public education.

The Libertarian/Republican interpretation of the constitutional authority to raise taxes for the general welfare flies in the face of the founders' defense of that constitutional authority to tax for the general welfare. The founders argued that *"promoting the general welfare"* authorized the government *to collect taxes toThe Libertarian/Republican interpretation in the Constitution.*

Those taxes were to be collected for the general welfare, *not an individual citizen's personal financial choices. The founders were clear about this governmental power to tax for the general welfare. What they, the founders, did not agree to, or sanction, is taxation without representation.*

Local school boards are comprised of our community's *elected representatives.* As such, they answer to the community's voters. The Constitution does not speak about handing governance of a public good over to unelected corporate boards overseeing an educational service provider controlled by a CEO owner.[1]

Efforts by the charter industry to seek out access to local educational funding sources are the next phase in this threat to local control. This charade is referred to as *"true backpack funding"* in the literature put out by charter advocacy groups. Statewide property taxes used to finance charter contracts are manifestations of this usurping of local control, as the state, not the community, decides how to use taxes that the state will collect on local citizens' private property.

This type of tax on local property constitutes taxation without representation *at the local level.* It also robs those communities of their voice in public education in those communities. Arguing that we elect our state government legislators ignores the fact that local control is being usurped and bypassed when the state contracts out educational services, *in many cases to out-of-state and multinational corporations.*

The state and federal government's ability to tax for the public welfare is the source of the "contracted" funds those private businesses are accessing as "private contractors" of educational services. We expand further on the concept of taxation for the general welfare. This ability to tax for common defense[2] and public welfare was defended in the Federalist Papers, particularly in FP #40, which is cited here:

> Some, who have not denied the necessity of the power of taxation, *have grounded a very fierce attack against the Constitution, on the language in which it is defined.* It has been urged and echoed, that the power "to lay and collect taxes, duties, imposts, and excises, to pay the debts, *and provide for the common defense and general welfare of the United States,"* amounts to an unlimited commission to exercise every power which may be alleged to be necessary for the *common defense or general welfare.*

No stronger proof could be given of the distress under which these writers labor for objections, than their stooping to such a misconstruction.

The Federalist Papers' authors then provided a counterpoint to those arguing that the common welfare is not something that taxes can or should be collected for. Their argument goes after the frivolous claims that taxing for this purpose will destroy other individual liberties.[3]

> Had no other enumeration or definition of the powers of the Congress been found in the Constitution, than the general expressions just cited, the authors of the objection might have had some color for it; though it would have been difficult to find a reason for so awkward a form of describing an authority to legislate in all possible cases. A power to destroy the freedom of the press, the trial by jury, or even to regulate the course of descents, or the forms of conveyances, must be very singularly expressed by the terms "to raise money for the general welfare."

Misconstructions were used then, and misconstructions regarding what constitutes a free and appropriate education for the general welfare are being used now.

You do not contract out the general welfare in a republic. The government's role is to tax for and to *provide for the general welfare, not subcontract it out.*

When services are legitimately "contracted out," the government's role is to monitor the financial aspects of that contractor's billing and related party transactions; that is, there are regulations and rules regarding how the tax-sourced funds can be used.

The second paragraph in this section of Federalist Paper #40 is a tongue-in-cheek debunking by the founders of the "arguments" used to question the Constitution's use of the term "general welfare." The authors of this Federalist Paper were reacting to claims that providing for the general welfare with taxpayer funds was *fiscal overreach by the government.* We would be wise to remember that the first part of the phrase in this article is, *"provide for the common defense."*

PRIVATIZATION CREEP

In an age when the United States is continuing to use "contracted" security forces as a replacement for our armed forces, the creep of private ownership through contracted services is steadily increasing.

If teachers and education can be a contracted service, then why not fire and police services? Privatized prisons are now being abandoned or regulated by many states because they, state legislatures, have learned from their free-market mistakes.

Charter contracting needs to come under *the same fiscal scrutiny* as road contracts. Local control by locally elected boards needs to be reestablished. This is a true conservative approach.

We do not have to guess what Ronald Reagan would say about this. Mr. Reagan was firmly in the camp of local control of education. The 1984 Republican Platform[4] under Ronald Reagan included a position on public education, while the platform spoke about "choice." The platform also called for *local control:*[5]

> The key to the success of educational reform lies in accountability: for students, parents, *educators, school boards, and all governmental units*. All must be held accountable in order to achieve excellence in education. *Restoring local control of education* will allow parents to resume the exercise of their responsibility for the basic education, discipline, and moral guidance of their children.

There is no local control in a charter contractor's provision of services. The state and federal government have been experimenting since 1991 with a "blended model" of the economic theory of action captured in these party-based political positions.

Politically, Democrats have also bought in to the idea of charter schools and "choice." This buy-in was clearly demonstrated to the author while he was working with Senators Judd Gregg and Ted Kennedy, who were the chairs of the Senate Education Committee in the late 1990s. This occurred when our New Hampshire district, in partnership with other NH districts and colleges, applied for and received funding to start Public School Choice in rural New Hampshire (1999).

The road we are currently on leads to full privatization of "public education" unless we, the people, either vote with our feet or elect legislators who value and defend locally controlled public education.

The phrase "Starving the beast of public education," and the Libertarian Party's stated agenda[6] to make parents responsible for paying for their children's education, are left out of the brochures, ads, and websites promoting the industry's efforts to privatize public education. These stated positions still underlie Libertarian platforms regarding education.[7]

It is time that we reassessed our assumptions that a free-market economic theory is the answer to promoting and providing for the public welfare. The economic theory in action is causing financial meltdowns in the charter industry and endangering all of our investments in our children's education.

It is a triple threat to our local communities' financial, political, and social capital.

Granting access to a deregulated, government-subsidized educational marketplace has financial, political, and social consequences.

A financial meltdown of a deregulated industry is one of the consequences.

NOTES

1. In old Westerns, the townspeople do not plan to open a private school run by a contracted service provider when the sheriff finally cleans out the outlaws. They build a town school. Why? To show that the town is now civil and civilized. The citizens have banded together for the public good.

2. Another use of our taxes for the common defense that is a slippery slope is the use of contractors for services previously performed by our armed forces.

3. The careful use of "freedom to choose" in literature supporting charters and vouchers plays on this. Jefferson was always clarifying the difference between *liberty*, which is guaranteed by the Constitution, and *freedom*, which he defined as being free from despotic restraints. Feedom to choose was always present, even prior to charter legislation. Responsibility to pay for that choice was a given part of that freedom to choose. See also: http://eyler.freeservers.com/JeffPers/jefpco26.htm.

4. http://www.presidency.ucsb.edu/ws/index.php?pid=25845.

5. President Reagan's enthusiastic support in selecting my fellow New Hampshire educator, Christa McAuliffe, was affirmation of his respect for the teaching profession: "One of America's finest contractors, a teacher."

6. https://lpedia.org/1980_National_Platform#4._Education.

7. http://www.ontheissues.org/Celeb/Libertarian_Party_Education.htm.

Chapter Sixteen

Market Meltdown

When confronted with the status of charter contractors' financials and the 43.5 percent failure rate[1] in Arizona charters since 1994, the industry's canned answer is, "That's how free markets work," followed by, "We designed it to work that way."

This is still the response in 2019, even though the industry itself predicted what it considered a high failure rate of 15 percent in the charter marketplace. *Twenty percent (82 sites) of those 434 failed schools closed during the school year.*

Unsustainable net losses lead to business failures. Bankruptcies do not respect state contracts to deliver on promised educational programs.

From fiscal year 2014[2] through fiscal year 2017, the statistics illustrated in figure 16.1 marked end-of-year financial losses at Arizona charter schools. The data is reported by sites, rather than by charter or by corporation. This is the same method used by the Arizona State Board for Charter Schools for listing and reporting on charter academic and financial performances. The number of sites in each category is tabulated in figure 16.1.

The sites represented are only those sites that are under the state charter board's control regarding financial and academic performance ratings.

Net losses are a "tell" in any business's fiscal data that the company is losing money.

As a reference, a continuing net loss that is greater than 10 percent of a public school's budget is cause for the state to step in and take over a "competition" district public school. Only eight districts in Arizona had a net loss in FY 2017. None of those districts had a net loss greater than $1M in FY 2017. One district, Murphy District, was taken over by the state in 2018 for its repeated net losses. *A district that has had past issues is the Roosevelt District in Phoenix.*

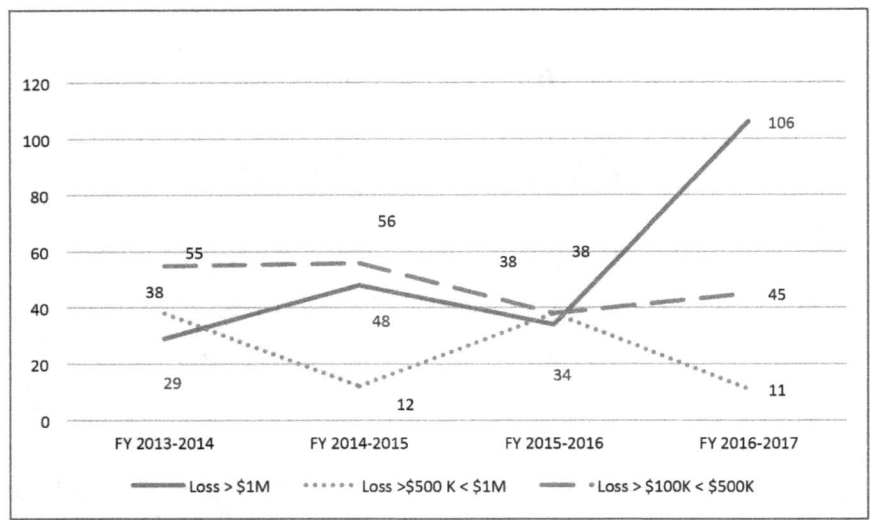

Figure 16.1. Net Losses at Arizona Charters FY 2014–2017
Source: Collated ASBCS Audit data on Revenues less Expenditures from FY 2014 to FY 2017

A total of 106 charters, or 20 percent of all charter sites, had a $1M+ loss in FY 2017. Critics who complain that our research does not look at the same financial issues in districts are misdirecting the public. It does.

Economically, the charter industry holds property and assets that are rife with upside-down property holdings (under-water mortgages and long-term debt on those overleveraged properties). Adding to this financial stress on the company's revenues and cash flow are *committed long-term leases.*[3]

THE ISSUE WITH LONG-TERM LEASES WITH A RELATED PARTY

Long-term leases are typically held by, and paid to, related real estate companies that own the charter's physical assets.

We do note there is also an overleveraging of short-term debt and student count estimates (estimated student counts that do not materialize but were used to obtain and guarantee the short-term loans). We did not count this type of debt in our analysis.

Evidence of a business financing strategy called "factoring" was noted. Factoring is used to leverage the school's accounts receivable. In the case of charters, this "receivable" means student ADM funding from the state.

The noted financial collapses are harbingers of what is to come. Grand Canyon Institute's metadata can now be used to accurately predict which charters are going to fail financially within two years, based on current and historic data trends. The data has been shared with the state charter board.

The corporate boards, which are often legally stacked with related parties, business associates, and unelected "governing boards" of these private enterprises, are rubber-stamping this economic activity. There is no requirement in charter law that the charter holder or corporate board member have either a business or an educational pedigree.

This lack of expertise is the equivalent of the state and federal governments contracting out for medical services to firms with no doctors or medical practitioners. When CEOs began running HMOs and hospitals with business efficiency, we received a different version of what used to be personalized health care. Doctors and patients were no longer making medical decisions.

While the same statement could be used as an argument regarding *elected school boards* (i.e., members do not have to hold a degree or a qualifying business certificate), those boards' agents must be certified as qualified practitioners. This standard also applies to the CFO (chief financial officer, i.e., business manager) of a district. The superintendent is the agent of those elected school boards (the CEO), a position that requires specific educational and financial training and expertise. Business managers (CFO) at public schools also must be state-certified; many hold MBAs.

The "governing boards" that are approving the budgets at charters are not elected. Cross-checking the "governing board" lists[4] with the corporate board names reveals that both boards are often composed of the same members.

In a large number of cases, corporate board members were also doing business with the charter school *or were employed by the charter school*. This can be a cost-saving move toward efficiency; however, six-figure payments to corporate board members are noted in the data.

This practice, hiring board members, is a clear conflict of interest in the competing sector, public district schools. School boards in districts are typically uncompensated or minimally compensated. Conflicts of interest are quickly pointed out by other board members and defined in writing in board policies.

When the industry cites the role of the "governing board" to oversee budgets, it fails to note *that in only 23 percent of the cases are these boards composed of independent, unrelated people.*[5] The use of employees to fill these roles is the norm witnessed by this author in the field and evident in the data.

This type of governance structure puts the employees in the untenable position of having to place a "check" on their employer's business practices based on the limited information to which they are allowed access.

What about the claims that a free market will correct itself based on economic performance? First of all, the market is neither "free" nor "open." It is also a government-subsidized market. Debt is propping up those businesses, with net losses noted in the graph on net losses. Debt is funded by tax-free bonds.

The author has heard this refrain regarding self-correcting markets in various forms when these financial issues have been raised with charter advocacy groups: "Why would the libertarian in me worry about a private business taking on those financial risks?"

Translation of the comment: "The free market will deal with these financial issues." The logic used to justify this stance is that charter owners are taking the financial risk and that educational free markets will correct themselves based on academic performance.

In reality, charter holders *are taking the same personal economic risks that the "CEOs" in the last market meltdown were taking.* That is, *none*.

Deregulation (eliminating the fiscal controls present in school districts) holds charter owners and charter authorizers harmless from "good faith" financial decisions. In this worldview, profiteering is celebrated as a reward for "innovative financial" thinking.

Researchers questioning those ill-gotten gains are termed "un-American" or "socialist" when they point out the vast real estate holdings and the distributions taken by for-profit firms in the market. This defensive and offensive posture implicitly links pure capitalism to what it means to be an American. Those remarks confuse an economic theory of action, capitalism, with our political system, which is a democratic republic.

The country's experience with deregulation and "free markets" in the last financial meltdown should be informing our decision making regarding how our public funds are being used. Decision making should not be ruled by an assumption that the economic theory regarding free markets is failsafe. *It isn't.*

After the last market meltdown, the public asked, "Who is being held responsible for these financial failures?" Answer: No one.

The market rules made most of what was done in the last deregulated real estate and investment markets "legal." Bonuses were paid to CEOs while repossessions and under-water properties[6] were financially ruining the common citizen.

A 43.5 percent fiscal failure rate *is not a market correction*. It is a *flashing red light on the financial dashboard indicating that we have been duped again into trusting a deregulated "free market."* This time around, the free-market services are being funded and paid for with taxpayer funds for public education, *not private capital from private investors*. Turning up the rhetoric radio to drown out the engine noises is not solving the underlying problem.

The capital in this "capitalistic" model is coming from taxpayers. The real financial capital markets referred to in capitalist economic theory are capitalizing on that taxpayer-funded capital by lending the industry ever-increasing sums of money at junk bond rates. This is done using tax-free bonds, a form of state and federal subsidy of the charter industry's debt.

This is not how a capitalist free market is supposed to be funded.

Who stands to gain from this market churn? Answer: mega charter corporations and the junk bond markets.

Who is funding the charter and voucher advocacy groups pushing and enabling this privatization agenda?

The funding of the *American Legislative Exchange Council* (ALEC), which touts itself as the largest "membership association of state legislators," *is not coming from the legislative body members it represents*. It is readily apparent that only 10 percent of ALEC's operational expenses come from legislator dues. The rest is from investors who are intent on privatizing government contracts. *This private club for legislators is 90 percent paid for by corporate donors with a financial and political stake in the privatization of public education.*

These corporate donors are eager to see the privatization of public education, or its complete replacement with private schools and contracted educational services. The motivation behind this capital investment is political and economic gain, not the public good. The size of this market is attracting the predators.

Public education represents a $650 billion acquisition target—a target market ripe for a hostile corporate takeover. Hostile because it seeks to destroy that which it is replacing—publicly funded education in a republic. Ripe because of the careful discrediting of public education by those seeking to privatize education. ALEC describes itself with the following quote on its publicly available web pages. The byline reads: "Who is ALEC?"

> The American Legislative Exchange Council (ALEC) is America's largest nonpartisan, voluntary membership organization of state legislators dedicated to the principles of *limited government, free markets* and federalism. ALEC is comprised of nearly one-quarter of the country's state legislators and stakeholders from across the policy spectrum. ALEC members represent more than 60 million Americans and provide jobs to more than 30 million people in the United States.

The results of these limited government free markets in table 16.2 show the ever-growing deficient financial results of that philosophy in the number-three ranked state for charter and voucher friendliness, Arizona.

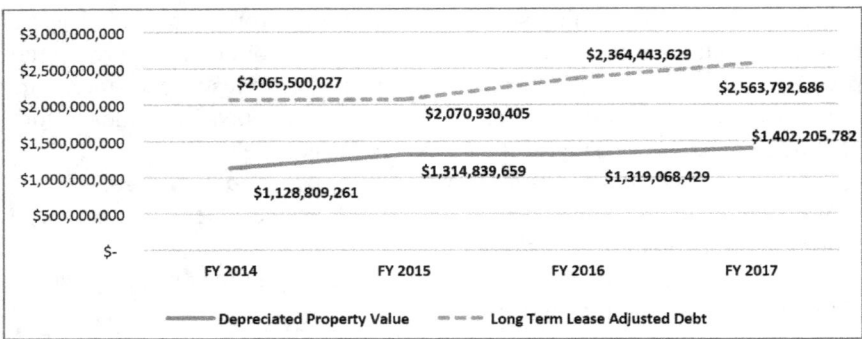

Figure 16.2. Charter Depreciated Property Value and Long-Term Lease Adjusted Debt
Source: Audited Property and Asset statements and IRS form 990 data from Nonprofit Charters from FY 2014 to FY 2017

At the end of fiscal year 2017 there was a *shortfall of $1,161,586,904* between the amount of property held by charters and the long-term debt and commitments on those properties. Conservative estimates based on available property transactions will show this figure at −$1.5 billion in FY 2019 as the data tracks five multimillion refinancing deals during FY 2018 and FY 2019.

Long-term debt is consuming charters' contracted service payments from the state. *It is also being collected by the debt holders prior to the money reaching the charter contractors.* This is done through financial *intercepts* that capture the funds coming from taxpayer sources. The bonds underwriting

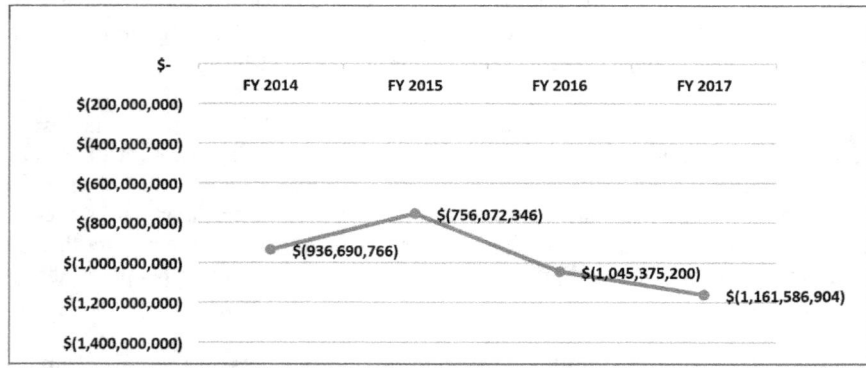

Figure 16.3. Underwater: Property Values—Long-Term Lease-Adjusted Debt FY 2014 to FY 2017
Source: FY 2014–2017 Collated Depreciated Property Values and Long-Term Lease-Adjusted Debt of Charters from Audits and Form 990

this long-term lease-adjusted debt are being guaranteed by the backpacks full of cash coming from the state.

Long-term leases with related parties holding the property debt commit the charter school to paying that subsidiary company's long-term debt with payments the charter makes on the committed leases. Payments that the charter is committed to by long-term lease contracts. In a free market this means that the firm holding the property can make money on the lease. This is a fair and normal free-market proposition, *except when those long-term leases are excessive.*[7]

This is the case with many of the related party long-term leases. Long-term debt is adjusted for these *committed* long-term leases on a financial statement. The data accumulated for these reports had to ensure that long-term lease debts were not added to long-term bond debt. A painstaking process of going through the IRS 990 data on nonprofit charters and the audits produced the results shown in this work. The data referred to in this chart *undercounts the debt-to-property issue*. Depreciation expenses were accommodated in our model.

How did our state and federal legislators get us into this financial fix?

Who is ALEC?

NOTES

1. Four hundred thirty-four sites out of 1,005 opened in June 2018. Source: Collated data on closures from ASCB site and additional data from Ed Reform reports.

2. School Fiscal Year 2014 is school year 2013–2014. The denotation of the Fiscal Year is the year the school year ended.

3. This lease commitment is referred to as a long-term debt "lease adjustment" when a financial analysis of long-term debt includes all long-term debt factors. It is listed as a "Commitment" on audit documents, as it must be paid.

4. The use of employees as governing board members puts the employee in the untenable position of voting to check the owner's power. This dynamic was witnessed by the author at several charters where he served on the governing board. This arrangement provides limited checks and balances.

5. All of the Arizona charter board members listed in public documents were evaluated using this criteria.

6. For all that this was touted as a business model, the claims that bonuses for teachers or high-performing administrators were driven by free-market economic theory were only borne out in one audit during the 2014 fiscal year. In several cases, teacher performance pay given to the charter contractor to reward teacher performances was used for other purposes, with one school taken to court over the issue in FY 2018.

7. *Fair* in our analysis means that the split between what the company is paying out in debt on the property and what it is charging for a lease is under 15 percent.

Chapter Seventeen

Controlling the Nation's Educational Agenda

Like the Know-Nothing party of the 1840s through the 1850s, the American Legislative Exchange Council (ALEC) is influencing political leaders at the state and federal levels in an effort to control and change the republic's social and educational agenda.

In an April 24, 2012, *Washington Post* article, Rachel Weiner identified the origin and composition of the original ALEC organization: "ALEC was formed in 1973 by conservative activists Lou Barnett and Paul Weyrich (who also founded the Heritage Foundation), along with then-State Rep. Henry Hyde (R-Ill.) and other Republican legislators."

The goal: "To bring conservative economic policy ideas to the state and local level."

A special report by PR Watch on ALEC's Funding and Spending provides the details of this organization, noting that, "Since CMD [The Center for Media and Democracy] first exposed ALEC in 2011, *more than 100 corporations have dropped ALEC, including Ford, Coca-Cola, Wal-Mart, General Electric, and Google.*"

As a result of that ongoing investigation and other reporting, CMD is often contacted by whistleblowers wanting to make a difference. CMD has also researched the array of groups that are part of ALEC, including numerous Koch[1]-funded entities and national and state "think tanks" that are affiliated with the State Policy Network.

Legislation encouraged and lobbied for by this group and charter advocacy associations has led to the current misguided rules of the game behind the privatization effort.

Diane Ravitch, a respected educational historian and former assistant secretary of education, sounded the alarm about the privatization movement in

2013 with her book *Reign of Error: The Hoax of the Privatization Movement and the Danger to America's Public Schools.*

The outrage from the public when the press exposes charter school practices that push the limits of legitimate business practices is well-documented in the literature.

The party line is that comparing district financial requirements to the financial practices at charters ignores the fact that these entities consider themselves private businesses operating with a contract with the state to provide *educational services.*

The privatization industry reminds us that they, charter schools, are businesses. As such, they are not public institutions, even though they describe themselves as public schools that do not charge tuition. The public is told to focus on academic results, not finances, when the topic of financial issues is brought up.

The papers that back up the financial statements made in this book focus on the red flags in the financials and identify issues with the *business* practices causing those red flags. Links to those reports are provided in the reference sections of this book and in endnotes. This work and those reports quantify the scale and nature of these financial losses to the tax-sourced funding of public education. *This type of analysis is a fiscally conservative approach to school financial discussions.*

This telling also includes examples *in which charters are fulfilling and delivering on their espoused economic theories of action.* It debunks some of the data that is generalized regarding the industry as a whole when questionable practices are exposed,[2] that is, trotting out and citing examples from the 23 percent of charters that have already been identified as ethically carrying out their contracts for educational services. This is done in an attempt to draw attention away from the data that represents 77 percent of the market.

The records on actual financial performance, often in a public form that was "a riddle wrapped in an enigma,"[3] have been decoded for this analysis. An intensive process of financial analysis began in 2012.

To their credit, the Arizona State Board for Charter Schools has been responsive to critiques regarding its financial and academic data reporting. The data that this board controls, the annual audits, is now much easier to access. The same board is working on several of the financial issues that this work speaks to. Good for them.

Economic theories of action applied to market sectors that are designed to support the general welfare should be called into question when financial results do not match the intentions stated in the theory.

The market is not self-correcting.

Bureaucracy analogies regarding district politics have been replaced by real economic oligarchies and monopolies cashing in on public education in the charter sector. Gandhi would have called this "commerce without morality" or "politics without principle"—two of his seven social sins. Greed, of course, is one of the seven deadly sins.

Greed in a capitalist economic model is equated with "good," as espoused by Gordon Gecko in the movie *Wall Street*. He famously said, "Greed, for the lack of a better work, is good." That fictionalized character paraphrased Friedman's thought on the social responsibility of businesses, that is, that they have *no social responsibility* (Friedman, 1970). Businesses are responsible to shareholders and owners, not society.

Do we still really believe that this is how public schools should be run—like these types of capitalist businesses? Or do we believe that businesses do have a social responsibility when they are operating in an area that is considered a public good?

At a gut level, this type of economic thinking applied to education "feels" wrong.

Hayek, another free-market proponent, wrote about the differences between laws we naturally obey and legislation that forces obedience to a legislative decree (Dyzenhaus & Poole, 2015). Natural laws are the ones being violated when financial "malfeasance" at charter schools (and district schools) occurs.

Our revulsion regarding what we have discovered when commerce is engaged in without morality comes from our ideals regarding how money should be spent on our children. Our expectation is that those tax-sourced funds are going toward educating those students, not profiteering. *An economic model doesn't guarantee that our expectations will be met.*

NOTES

1. Koch was the vice-presidential candidate for the Libertarian Party in the 1980s.

2. For example, citing mom-and-pop charter holders, married couples who put their life savings into a charter that now has an "A" rating and is financially sound. The surprise to these promoters of the status quo is when the author names the outlier school that the advocacy group is talking about. Fact: These "great charters" constitute 23 percent of the market. Free markets are not eliminating academically failing online schools that have changed their school types to alternative schools to avoid scrutiny. An academic rating of NR (Not Rated) is listed for 35 percent of the charters in Arizona. Source: Arizona Charter Associations' website August 17, 2018. Cited in Grand Canyon Institute's third paper, Red Flags: Overleveraged Properties and Assets. www.grandcanyoninstitute.org.

3. The phrase "a riddle wrapped in an enigma" was used by Winston Churchill when asked to describe the USSR.

Chapter Eighteen

The Economics of School Choice

Carol Hoxby,[1] a noted economist and educator, asked this question at the start of an *Economics Journal* piece she wrote in 2013, "The Economics of School Choice" (Hoxby, 2003):

> What does it mean to perform an economic analysis of school choice? It does not mean that the authors in this volume are interested only in the financial aspects of school choice. The authors are deeply interested in (and analyze) many non-financial aspects of choice, including student achievement, parental satisfaction, school segregation, mainstreaming of disabled children, and parents' choice of where to live.
>
> What it does mean is that the authors rely on methods that were originally developed for the purpose of economic analysis. (In fact, when I refer to "economists," I refer to people who practice such methods—thereby including some people who are not card-carrying economists.)

The author of this work is not what Hoxby refers to as a "card-carrying economist."[2] The financial and economic expertise obtained from a life in public, charter, and business enterprises, along with over two thousand hours of school law, finance, and management courses/workshops, as well as forty-five years of experience, inform this work.

Hoxby's works have informed this analysis. Her readings were chosen because Hoxby performs what is referred to as a factor analysis on the data she looks at and relates this to the non-financial aspects of this issue.

The author is a *research practitioner*. That approach and mindset have the added advantage of assessing that data with a tacit understanding of the factors impacting that data (Virginia Polytechnic Institute and State University College of Architecture and Urban Studies, 2000).

Reflection on that tacit understanding enables a research practitioner to read any discussions regarding public education by paying attention to subsidiary details that the practitioner recognizes as significant factors. That is, it enables him or her to understand the myriad factors impacting the raw data being presented. An example of that process follows:

While researching a passage by Dr. Friedman[3] discussing how public school spending and overhead dramatically increased in the mid-1970s, I noticed that a *key federal educational policy factor* in those increases was ignored by Dr. Friedman, an economist.

Nowhere in that "analysis" is there any mention of Public Law 94-142, which added all of the special education children in the country to the public school system's mission. These children, and the mandates to locate them via child- find[4] efforts, added an entirely new group (ages 3 to 22) to the nation's public school mandates.

Educational factors matter when one is analyzing data on educational costs. Experience in the field of education allows the practitioner to pay attention to the subsidiary details that influence the numbers in the data. An additional edge is gained by being an insider at both charter and district schools.

Lived experiences in small charters, online charters, and large charter companies have led to this book. This practical experience included starting district and then independent charters in New Hampshire and ten years of working at a management level as a corporate officer (and on corporate boards) in for-profit and nonprofit charters in Arizona.

Ralph Waldo Emerson and Henry David Thoreau had a greeting they used after they had been apart for any length of time: "What has become clearer to you since last we met?"

Knowing that the question would be asked inspired and impelled both men to reflect on their experiences and how those experiences shaped their thinking. Socrates put the power of a reflective life succinctly: "The unexamined life is not worth living."

Education, whether in the classroom, at church, or in our public lives, affects our worldview. It is not a waste of time to ponder what lessons we are teaching our children about life in a republic and our duties to one another as citizens.

Social losses to our community occur when the "best and brightest parents" choose to move their children to a charter or private placement. We, as a society, collectively lose those parents' voices in our public schools.

This loss is felt by the community, and more importantly, by the children who would have benefited from learning from their peer group. This belief system informed the author's family decisions to keep his children at their local public school even though a scholarship to a private academy was available.[5] Those children are highly successful professionals today.[6] More importantly, they are actively involved with their communities, socially and politically. That is, they are engaged citizens in our democratic republic. They also know how to work with the whole spectrum of the workforce in their chosen fields. The Lion's Club motto—"Not above you, nor beneath you, but with you"—beautifully sums up this relationship of citizens in a republic.

Personal knowledge[7] comes from a tacit understanding of all of the factors a person is observing in practice. This knowledge, combined with experiences garnered as owner of both small and large businesses, responsible for payrolls and bottom lines, informs my discussion.

Charter advocates often critique former district administrators for "thinking like a district."

The thinking in this analysis was done from a business perspective.

The mindset is that of a business professional looking at financial results, not the intentions, of choice economic theory. Most importantly, this presentation is also the result of thinking like an American educator with practical experience in public schools, public charter schools, *and businesses*, all of which inform that thinking.

While we must compete economically in the world, *our educational efforts should be about educating our citizens about what it means to be an American. Districts and charters often lose track of this primary mission of an American school.*

Schooling Alone is a call to action similar to the one voiced in *Bowling Alone* by Robert Putnam, in which he decried the loss of social capital in American public life. The insidiousness of this radical reshaping of our public school financial model is also destroying local political capital. This social and political loss is a threat to our democracy.

If the current practices are left unchecked, they will also continue to deplete the financial capital that we have invested in our schools. This effort is designed to alert the public about what is, in effect, a hostile business takeover of our local community's public schools, a takeover enabled and sponsored by state and federal legislation that *intentionally removed* local control of education from our democratic republic's communities. Enough already.

Our community's schools have become the privatized "my" charter schools of the charter businesses contracted by the majority of states that have taken the charter route.

When interviewing citizens for this research work, the first question the author asked was this: "Who owns charter school facilities?" The majority of respondents believed that they, the public, owned those properties. A false premise.

While inside and outside of the industry, the concerns and information garnered for this report were shared by the author with the charter industry, politicians, and state agencies. The response of the leading advocacy group for charters in Arizona was one sentence: "What you have told us about is all legal."

The efforts to share the data with this group are documented in our archives. A "see no evil, hear no evil" mentality prevents these organizations from really looking at data that contradicts the party line. They are correct about one thing: Everything described is legal under existing charter legislation. But is it ethical?

An Arizona legislator's comment on the 43.5 percent failure rate at charters was, "We designed the legislation to work that way."

One is reminded of a common Baby Boomer refrain from the 1960s: "I meant to do that."

Therein lies the issue. *Denial.*

Denial that the central economic theory driving the "school choice" model could be mistaken when applied to a government-funded public good is blinding charter advocacy groups to the financial time bombs present in the data.

Ideology and rhetoric about free markets is also blinding our public discourse regarding how to provide a free and appropriate American education to our children. It is those children and their children who will bear the costs of this march of folly.

Good people can be divided by politics as they settle into opposing camps. Sound financial management of taxpayer-funded resources is not, nor should it be, a liberal versus conservative issue. The political and religious elements of the discussion regarding an American public education are following past patterns of behavior that are predictable and, in the end, will be divisive *if we allow them to continue unabated*. We can use our reason to get past the emotional rhetoric[8] used by both sides of the public school versus contracted charters and vouchers issue.

Kurt Vonnegut said it best when talking about why we are here on Earth: "We are here to help each other get through this thing, whatever it may be" (Vonnegut, 1997). Education is about helping one another understand and be a part of our American democracy. Vonnegut always credited the teachers at his Indianapolis public schools for his ability to write.[9] Vonnegut was always an avid supporter of our public schools despite the fact that some school boards banned (and some actually burned) his book *Slaughterhouse Five*.

At present, there are reasonable and good people who are either missing, or deliberately ignoring, the financial warning signals in the data. The red light is on. The engine of democracy, an educated citizenry, is going to seize up because we are ignoring the "check engine" light by blithely believing that a financial free market is self-correcting.

The light isn't going out on its own. Engines of real educational innovation and academic performance are being financially destroyed in the process. We've seen these types of red lights before.

This is like what occurred in the savings and loan disasters, the junk bond crash, and the mortgage failures of 2007 and 2008, when the financial practices were condoned by a "deregulated free market economic approach." Charter schools' financials are now critically stressed due to constant refinancing and re-bundling of debt.

Children are being treated as "backpacks full of cash" in this model and as revenue assets backing up the financing of this market's debt. The intentional exemption of charter holders from financial rules and regulations that apply to districts seals the deal given to charter holders and voucher programs in legislation based on a free-market economic theory of action.

The economic model is not working. It is not working in the same way that it did not work in other deregulated financial markets. We have been sold another deregulation and free-market economic theory scenario as a solution set to all of our academic and financial problems in the education market. This time the "market" is capitalized by public taxes raised to provide for the general welfare.

How did we fall for this solution set? We fell for false analogies.

NOTES

1. Hoxby does an excellent job reporting on other economists' thinking and influence regarding "school choice" and the free-market approach to education. We acknowledge these economic influences in our discussion but center on the familiar theories and writings of Nobel Prize winners. Only Milton Friedman was awarded the Nobel.

2. Author's note: The use of the word *socialist* to discredit any free-market critique of the economics behind school choice is neither helpful nor productive.

3. A comparison of capitalism and freedom between school spending and the increase in spending on the "socialistic" British health care system was being made. The same comment regarding education as a "socialistic" endeavour was made in *Free to Choose* in 1980 (Friedman, 1980; Friedman, 1982).

4. Child Find is a requirement of Public Law 94-142, which created a mandate for districts to locate children who would fall under the rules of PL 94-142. In one NH district, 94-142 caused an immediate increase of $250,000 for a student who was born with an undeveloped brain, that is, a brainstem was the only part of the child's brain that developed during gestation. While this is an extreme case, many of the children who were formerly in hospital placements were now a part of the educational system's fiscal responsibility. Local Educational Agencies, LEAs, work with State Educational Agencies, SEAs, to pay for these students' educational costs.

5. A merit scholarship due to their outstanding performances on advanced placement tests.

6. As a member of the local Lion's Club for thirty years, the author started each meeting with the Lion's greeting: "Not above you nor beneath you, but with you."

7. Michael Polanyi coined the terms *personal knowledge* and *tacit knowledge*. See Polanyi, 1952, 1958.

8. See Jonathan Haidt's *The Righteous Mind: Why Good People Are Divided by Politics and Religion*.

9. Vonnegut's support of public education is found in many of his writings and his college speeches. He never graduated from college and once was turned down for a teaching position at a community college.

Chapter Nineteen

False Analogies

Charter and privatization advocacy groups often use analogies to justify the contractual nature of charter agreements. The logic used is that those chartering agreements authorize charter holders to provide the state with educational services for a set fee per child plus any additional funding the state provides. In other words, education is now a purchased service.

The use of analogies is another way charter and voucher advocates have of justifying the deregulated use of public funds. The logic used for this justification is that once those funds have been paid to the charter contractor, they constitute a *payment for services*. The analogies allow for a quaint, quick, logical-sounding soundbite when the idea of contracting out government obligations is questioned.

The analogies used are a part of the ongoing effort to convince the public that this use of public funds to contract with a charter corporation is free-market business as usual. We are told that the charter (contractor) is taking all of the financial risks[1] and therefore the charter CEO should be able to reap financial rewards from this risk.

The problem with analogies taken at face value is that they often do not hold up to scrutiny. Several prime examples of this process follow.

"It's just like contracting out for road construction." A frequently used set of analogies regarding contracting educational services to private businesses compares it to contracting the construction of our public highways and municipal roads. Another analogy is made comparing this process to the construction of US Navy ships and military expenditures by private contractors. The argument states that these contractors own their equipment even though it was paid for with tax dollars. *The equipment, yes, but not the property.*

The analogies cited are used to defend the right of CEOs to profit from a financial relationship with the government and the right of the charter contractor to subcontract to other "educational management organizations, or EMOs." The defenders of the status quo use bookkeeping manipulation in order to state that the IRS status[2] of the related party subcontractor (as defined by IRS rules regarding related party transactions) *does not apply to the deregulated charter market.*

Nepotism and related party transactions that did not put more money back into the classroom for educational services occurred in 77 percent of the charters that were evaluated using IRS standards regarding related party transactions. That is, we let the related party figures stated in the audits stand, even when it was clear that a related party transaction had occurred and may have been contradicted by the IRS 990 statements. Cross-checking of audits with the IRS 990 was done for all 501 C 3 corporations.

The statutes on charter schools in most of the states with charters allow the company to use no-bid contracting and related-party transactions. This is all part of business as usual in the world of charter-contracted services.

Issues with the highway analogy abound. The analogy fails to mention *that the finished roads and the land those roads sit on do not belong to the contractor.*[3] *It also fails to note* that the maintaining of those public roads is done by government employees.

When that detail is mentioned in states where the property belongs to the charter holder, the charter industry's answer is that the buildings *do belong to the charter contractor, but the education now belongs to the child. This statement is followed by another explanation. We are told* the education was what the contract was for, *not the buildings.*

We accept this logic for this discussion. However, even when one lets that argument stand, there are too many other instances in which this analogy fails to pass muster.

Construction businesses doing business with the state and municipalities *borrow money at commercial rates for the equipment they purchase.* That equipment is their private property. Consideration of the contract's value to the company and the equipment costs go into those contractor commercial loans. They don't receive "extra funds" to cover their other costs of doing business.

Construction companies don't borrow from tax-free bond markets. Those tax-free bond markets are subsidized by the federal and state governments, which are giving up the revenues that the lenders would have paid in taxes.

Road contractors also don't collect fees on their construction contracts[4] year after year even though their product, the road, is still there. In other words, they can't set up a toll booth.

There are also strict guidelines regarding the materials and specifications for the road. Rules of the game apply to construction contracts.[5] *The rules regarding school construction have been deregulated in the charter markets.*

Construction companies do not resell the road to the state or another construction company once it is built. They may place a competitive bid on repairing the roads or on a rebuild. That new contract *is not guaranteed to go to the original builder*. The optimal word here is *bid*. The construction company has to bid on the contract. They don't receive a contract if they don't win the bid or if their previous work did not meet specifications.

Contracted construction companies' business headquarters and yards *are* the property of the company. In the free market, they may buy and sell these properties as they see fit. The contractors' private property and assets, *which they pay taxes on*, are theirs to keep and sell, *not the road they were contracted to build*.

Construction companies are not allowed to declare themselves nonprofits. They are real "for-profits." As such, they are subject to property taxes.

Yes, school district properties are not subject to property taxes. The difference is that the property of a district is owned by the taxpayers of that district *who do pay property taxes. In other words, they shouldn't be taxed again on property they own as citizens of that district.*

Nonprofit charters do not pay property taxes even though they are, by their own definition, contracted service providers who own those properties as private property. In Arizona, charter contracts include an extra $2,000+ per student for these expenses. This extra payment even goes, at a slightly reduced rate, to the online charters *that have no physical sites.*

By law, in the majority of states with charters, the property and assets belong to the charter holders. They are also, by law, free to encumber those assets to borrow money. The money they anticipate receiving for their students counts as a revenue asset in this convoluted equation.

Legislators with interests in the charter contracting business have answered that "We designed it to work that way" when asked about this financial arrangement. "Designed it that way" is correct.

That's why, when the public questions the transactions, the party line response is, *"That's how free markets work, and we are running our corporations as businesses."*

That's not really how free markets work.

The analogy regarding federal contracts on military equipment also fails to pass muster.

The ships the navy purchases from ship contractors say *United States Navy* on the side and are manned by our armed forces, who are government employees. There are naming protocols for ships and bases. In other words, the contractors don't name the ships after their companies.

The analogies coined by the "free market" promotors to justify education as a contracted service do not hold water. A deeply entrenched belief in an economic theory of action to solve our perceived and real educational issues is ingrained in our thought processes. That preconceived notion kicks in when we accept these faulty analogies at face value. We, the public, have fallen for a "bait and switch" tactic.

These same false analogies are trotted out after every new charter scandal. Isn't it time to question the logic here?

Why do we continue to fall for the same rhetoric by moving on until the next scandal hits the newspapers? Answer: We have been conditioned to think that deregulation solves things because a free market self-corrects.

We act like a gambler who remembers his wins but forgets his losses. The same factor of remembering the wins and forgetting the losses applies to how we think about the economy as a whole.

We are ignoring historical lessons about trusting a deregulated financial market.

Despite the economic crash of 2007–2008, the failure of the savings and loans market in the 1980s, the junk bond crisis in the 1990s, and the raiding of pension funds in the last century, Americans continue to believe in the idealized model we have of a deregulated "free market."

In the field of education, we have confused our love of democratic principles with this Pollyanna-like belief in a capitalist economic system as the solution set to all markets where there are monetary exchanges.

Public education is a public good. Like fire departments and police departments, school systems were designed to promote and provide for the common welfare.

The role of public schools is to provide the republic with educated citizens, not to make a profit. We don't expect our police or fire departments to be in the business of making money from their interactions with the public. When police personnel do so, they are rightfully referred to as "dirty cops."

Charters and private schools are intentionally designed to make a profit in a "free market." The economic theory is that if they don't satisfy market demand for academic quality, they will fail. The theory depends on us believing that when parents (consumers of educational services) are "free to choose," they will elect to move their children either to a district school or to another charter—that is, they will exit the school. The data from this market does not support the veracity of that exiting theory.[6]

One of the reasons for this mismatch between the financial data and the exiting theory postulated by the charter industry is that the public has been sold an idealized version of free-market economic theories *that neglects to provide the consumer with enough information, academic and financial, to make an educated choice based on solid evidence.* The model also assumes that all parents are acting like what Dewey refers to as "the best and brightest parents."

A simple test of what you really believe is to read the charter laws and replace the words relating to schools with the words *fire department, police department*, or *any branch of our armed services*. All of these "government" functions are there to protect and serve the citizens of our republic.

Do we really believe that private companies without financial oversight from an elected board or city council should be in charge of those functions of local government in a republic?

If our military was composed of contracted-service providers, we would call those contracted workers "mercenaries." Teachers are not mercenaries, nor should we treat them as such.

When our federal government contracted out our security forces in Iraq and Afghanistan, it did not "save money" or create efficiencies. Those contracted-service security personnel typically make $1,000 a day. We are not supporting our troops when we pay subcontractors to do jobs that they have volunteered to do for a fraction of the cost. The source of funding for both is our federal taxes. We are not supporting our teachers when we allow contractors for educational services to pay those teachers less than the market rate.

Do we really want our teachers to be hired subcontractors of our contracted educational service providers, rather than professionals who are *our* employees? School principals and teachers now answer to the charter contractor first, not the public. The logical consequence of a contracted educational system is that they—the teachers, aides, and principals—are now the subcontracted help of the contract-holding owner.

This stance was recently driven home by a charter holder's response to a reporter's question about his charter's finances: "I don't answer to you, I answer to the charter board." He, the charter holder, was legally correct. This treatise asks, "Did we, the public, really mean for that to be the case?" We weren't asked.

Charters are the result of legislation at the state and federal levels. Our political capital as a community has been usurped. It is costing us economically, and more importantly, it is destroying communities' political and social capital.

The idealized version of free markets comes from economists who believe in a purely capitalistic model, then apply that model to public education. That model's premise is that money and profits drive human intentions in a free market. The model asserts that the profit motive is the real reason people provide services and products to the consumer. It doesn't really work that way.

In any case, the model profit theory is clearly not being applied to the market's employees' financial aspirations in a capitalist economy. Those free-market employees, according to the same economic theory, should be operating in a capitalistic way also. The model would have us believe that teachers are working for the highest bidder in a profession that has severe shortages.

Shouldn't that mean that the best-performing charters and private schools should be competing for the top-tier teachers? If so, then why are charter teacher salaries and benefits woefully behind districts (15 to 20 percent lower)? What explains this un-capitalistic behavior on the part of our teachers?

When human beings decide to enter a service profession, their motivation isn't always monetary.[7] Teachers, police and fire personnel, and our troops are not motivated by the money they can make from their service to their communities and their country. They expect a living wage for that effort.

At this juncture, the defenders of the free-market economic model will trot out the standby claim that people who question the model are "socialists." This comes from a mindset that equates a capitalistic economy with a political democracy. It is also a throwback to McCarthyism and the era when the free-market educational theory originated.

The last five financial "scandals" involving charter contractors in Arizona totaled $70 million taken as "profits." This occurs in a state that "can't find the funds" to finance teacher raises. How can the profit-taking feel so wrong and at the same time be perfectly legal and justifiable under the free-market theory underlying the industry's economic model?

This tension between making profits and social justice has always been part of capitalism in a democracy.

NOTES

1. By registering as an LLC (Limited Liability Corporation) or as a C Corp, the owners' liabilities are limited to their businesses. That is, their personal funds are held harmless from bankruptcy proceedings. This is a standard practice in the business world.

2. For example, by claiming a lower percentage stake in the related party business, the owners of the charter can insist this is not a related party transaction because they are not the majority shareholder. Keeping the equity stake in the subsidiary company low says nothing about the profit that stakeholders can take from that company. The public has no access to the audits of these related party companies. Therefore, we recognize that our datasets undercounted the issues being discussed, because if the owner did not *declare* a related party transaction, we did not record one. This was the case in a company identified as an exemplar in the book *Carpetbagging America's Public Schools*. A deeper probe led to the realization that this "exemplar" had hidden its related party transactions in the manner described above. The same company pays retirement benefits for its management team, including ownership, and denies it to its

employees by leasing those employees from "an unrelated" firm that the owner has a minority stake in.

3. The government giveaway to railroads during the age of the "Robber Barons" included the land on either side of the tracks. Price fixing for rail services and other monopolistic practices that were taken on by Theodore Roosevelt are a historic example of why this type of giveaway of property and assets is not in the public's interest. The railways also saw consolidation of the market as several firms dominated this "free market." We tend to forget that the Interstate Commerce Act of 1887 was a Congressional reaction to the fact that states were not regulating the railroads.

4. Experimentation with "fees for HOV lanes" that allow the contractor to recoup the construction costs of the road via a usage fee has been spotty at best.

5. *The rules for road contracts in several municipalities in Arizona and other states were reviewed prior to this chapter being written. Those rules are posted on municipal web pages.*

6. See *Exit, Voice and Loyalty* (Hirschman, 1970) and *Who Chooses, Who Loses* (Fuller, 1997) for information regarding what drives decisions regarding parental "choice." Leaders at charters and districts would benefit from Hirshman's seminal work in this area. Also recommended are the works of Carol Hoxby regarding the economics of school choice.

7. Friedman's original discussions theorized that if nursing were paying more than teaching, then students would shift from a teaching degree to a nursing degree. While both are service professions, the jump to changing professions for financial gain does not hold up. You do not run into many people who will tell you, "I changed my program because I found out nurses make more than teachers." The "tell" in this argument is that both professions were predominantly female at the time. Sexism still permeates and impacts discussions regarding what teachers should be paid.

Chapter Twenty

Capitalism and Democracy

There has always been tension between our republic's economic model, capitalism, and our political model, a democratic republic. The tension comes from how both of these ideas work *in tandem* in a republic. In his bestselling book *Tailspin: The People and Forces behind America's Fifty-Year Fall—and Those Fighting to Reverse It*, Steven Brill articulates the reason for this tension:

> *There has always been an inherent tension in societies that are politically democratic and economically capitalist. The former is based on equality; the latter is fueled by the participant's dreams of accruing more wealth than the other guy. Maintaining political equality in a land of wealth inequality requires a delicate balance.*
>
> *If the forces of political equality prevail so totally that they do too much to equalize wealth, such as with confiscatory taxes, the incentives and energy of a capitalist system are eroded. If wealth inequality gets too extreme, the power of the wealthy can be deployed to erode democracy.* (Brill 2018)

AN ECONOMIC VERSUS A POLITICAL THEORY OF ACTION

The charter and voucher movements are founded on an economic theory of action applied to publicly funded education in a democratic republic. Politically this meant that decision making about public education shifted from the local level to the state. The model has also become politicized, with multiple political parties—Democratic, Republican, and Libertarian—participating in the legislative actions authorizing public funds to contract educational service providers.

The Libertarian Party, which has since backed away from Friedman's use of government funding to finance education in a democratic republic, wrote its seminal educational platform regarding public education in 1980. The vice-presidential candidate in that critical year was none other than David Koch, of the billionaire Koch brothers.

The euphemistic descriptions of charter schools promulgated by the National Conference of State Legislatures (ALEC) were designed to "ease" the public's perception about the real goals of the economic theory behind "school choice"—a purely capitalistic marketplace for educational services. Those goals were articulated in that 1980 Libertarian Party platform, which states the real goals of this movement regarding the education of children[1] in a republic.

The logical conclusions of enacting these policies are that individuals would be able to choose *whatever they could afford to pay for educational services*. Economic decisions regarding what you could afford to pay for education at the individual level would drive your consumer choices—a true capitalist model, driven by individual choice and the individual's ability to pay. We have evidence regarding how that model would work in the historical records of our republic.

HISTORICAL CONTEXT

The 1980 Libertarian educational platform was describing educational choice *as it existed in the United States prior to universal, taxpayer-funded public education (1919)*. The educational results of that model were terrible: the highest illiteracy rates among the general population in our republic's history, widespread poverty, and a low standard of living. There is a reason the first national political moves into education at the elementary and high school level were termed *national defense initiatives*.

Illiteracy plagued the nation's armed forces in the First and Second World Wars. Education and the taxes used to support it were purposely designed to promote the general welfare, *not individual economic choices*.

The words prior to *"the general welfare"* in the Constitution are related to our common defense, another area in which the country has debated who is responsible for paying the bills. There is a reason why a standing army and navy did not form immediately after the nation was founded. State and local militias are one of the reasons the Constitution's Second Amendment was written. It doesn't read *"a well-regulated national army."* It says, *"A well-regulated militia."*

Article I, section 8 of the U. S. Constitution grants Congress the power to "lay and collect Taxes, Duties, Imposts, and Excises, to pay the Debts and provide for the common defense and general Welfare of the United States."

Citizens of this country have always had the freedom to choose where they send their children for an education. The Libertarian education platform is describing the same "freedom to choose" that was available to all parents (again financially driven) to choose which type of school they sent their children to prior to 1994. In addition to this "choice," they also, after 1919, had a publicly financed choice of where to send their children to school.

The difference after 1994 was that in some states, charter and voucher laws allowed those parents the freedom to claim a government subsidy to finance that individual choice. That subsidy is paid out to private contractors from tax revenues. Isn't this what conservatives usually call an "entitlement mentality"? That is, "I am entitled to an educational choice that the general public pays for with their taxes."

The "government schools" system derided in this political platform came into play after mandatory schooling laws were enacted in all states in 1919. *Within a year, child labor laws were also enacted, encouraged by the burgeoning labor movement at that time.*

PERSONAL FINANCIAL RESPONSIBILITY IS AN AMERICAN VALUE

When choice advocates utter the words *"freedom to choose,"* they are describing a freedom that individual citizens *already have.* There is *nothing in the mandatory requirements to educate children* in the republic that prevents private citizens from choosing another form of education, *as long as they pay for it.*

This freedom also includes homeschooling, which is also a choice. States legislated homeschooling into mandatory education laws during the twentieth century. Funding homeschool parents for choosing to educate their children in isolation from the community is a misappropriation of taxpayer funds. Those taxpayer-sourced funds are being used to support an unregistered, unsupervised education provided by the parents. The new rules make access to some of those funds an entitlement. With whom is the educational contract made when tax dollars are paid out to homeschool parents?

When news stories include critiques of public figures sending their own children to private schools, that criticism is misplaced. Public schools were initiated to provide *every citizen* with an *equal opportunity* to obtain an education. A private school *choice was always an option. But who paid for that "consumer of educational services" choice was not.* Choices within the public school system were also covered under freedom of choice in this era.

The author's parents, who went to public schools in New Jersey during the 1920s, chose to send their five children and several foster children to private kindergarten and to Catholic schools for their elementary and high school programs. They paid for this choice. The freedom to choose a religious education was a given. They also contributed to funds designed to assist fellow parishioners who could not afford the tuition at those schools. The payment for that religious choice was a commitment to their religious community. The tuition fees were not tax-deductible at that time. Direct donations to our church were.

Their descendants chose public, private, and Catholic schools for their own children. All supported the public schools' tax-supported funding for the children in their larger communities. The pure capitalists in the lot have made fortunes by choosing fields that did not rely on government funding. The educators in the mix choose to work in public, private, charter, and child-care sectors. The example is given to show the social values that used to be transmitted by parents in the 1950s and 1960s.

"Choice," initiated in the 1990s, took a portion of the public funding to support a community's public education efforts and diverted it into an entitlement plan allowing parents to contract and register with private vendors. This entitlement is then paid for directly by the state with tax revenues.

Freedom is not free. In a free society, the cost of personal choices requires sacrifice and taking responsibility for one's own personal financial decisions.

THE "GREATEST GENERATION" GOT IT RIGHT

Public school systems in the United States were gifts to our country and communities from the Greatest Generation, a generation whose education and ability to compete was belittled in the press in the 1930s (Bracey, 1997). A little more respect for their wisdom and efforts to establish public schools is in order.

The Greatest Generation knew and understood the realities of the "good old days" of public education. They were born after mandatory education laws went into effect in 1919. When they returned from the Second World War, they dedicated their time and effort as school board members, teachers, and parents to make *public schools in their communities a center of public life.*

They were active members in civic organizations, devoted to serving needs in their communities. This was the generation that *did not bowl alone*, Robert Putnam's stand-in metaphor for our current loss of civic engagement. They bowled in leagues and coached children in their neighborhood leagues for free. Sports teams were sponsored by civic organizations that paid for uniforms and equipment for the children on their communities' teams.

This volunteerism and civic engagement ensured every child a chance to play, not a guarantee of athletic success. In a word, the adults at the time were what used to be termed "civic-minded." They took pride in their community and their involvement in that community.

Their efforts to provide educational opportunities and to fund public education *in their communities* are being dismantled at the state and federal levels under the guise of "freedom of choice." Schooling alone means that our citizens have less and less in common with their fellow community members.

There are even fewer reasons to put down our cell phones and engage with our communities. We have stopped rooting for the home team.

Who is the "home team" when there are twenty high schools in a small town?

Where do you go for a high school reunion when your charter contractor's school goes out of business?

Public schools bind a community together.

Communities need all of the talents that their inhabitants bring to the table, not just those of the academic standouts in the crowd. The bell curve is not some made-up statistical fluke. Our children are all talented, but in different ways. Friday night lights, where the town cheers for its home team, are *unifying communal events*.

Similarly, the importance of the arts in our social lives *cannot be overstated*. It is not a frill. High school bands provide communities with sources of pride during parades and memorial gatherings. All of these communal events transmit our culture and values to our children.

Our volunteer armed service members overwhelmingly come from high schools that were geared toward their communities and devotion to those communities and, by extension, their country. Combat veterans' devotion to their unit first and the soldier next to them in line reflects this need and our inborn desire for unit cohesion.

Police departments, fire departments, first responders, and all of the workers in our communities are made up of everyday average citizens. Uncommon valor is a common virtue in this segment of our population. Communities are the political and social units of which family units are a part. Valor is our way of naming service and dedication to our fellow Americans.

American schools are not just about academic performance. They are about educating Americans about what it means to be a participating member of a democratic republic.

Even when one looks at only the pure academic data, the results do not justify the financial, political, and social capital that is lost when we school alone.

We have been sold a lie about our children's educational performance. Gerald Bracey debunked the educational statistics used to justify a radical reframing of American public education (Bracey, 1997; Bracey, 2003; Bracey, 2004). It is telling that *American Heritage* magazine and the AARP published shortened versions of Bracey's work. Public education is part of our American heritage.

Can public education improve? Certainly, but we are not raising Japanese children, Indonesian children, or children of whatever is now the top academic country in the world. We are raising American citizens. There is a reason China, a high-performing academic juggernaut, studies our public schools and sends its children to American colleges. Our public schools produce innovators and entrepreneurs with a "can do" mindset.

We have let what Diane Ravitch refers to as "a billionaire boy's club" of successful businesspeople push for the privatization and dismantling of our public schools. Too many of them have the same motivation for this corporate takeover as Mr. Potter in Frank Capra's *It's a Wonderful Life*: a desire to capture a part of the billions of dollars we spend on public education, and the recognition of an opportunity for those who want a private education to be paid to use funding meant for the public welfare.

We are supposed to be getting educational excellence for this "regression to the myth" of privatized education.

The raw financial data from the last quarter of a century shows that there is no correlation between academic and financial performance. There are "A" schools that do not pass the charter board's financial performance expectations and multiple "D"-rated or Not Rated schools that are reaping excessive profits at their schools.

This use of an "Alternative School" designation bears repeating. *Thirty-five percent of charter sites in Arizona were not rated on the A through F system. Most of those schools declared themselves "Alternative Schools" the year prior to the academic accountability ratings going into effect.*

In the words of Milton Friedman: "One of the great mistakes is to judge policies and programs by their intentions rather than their results." This treatise deals with the social, political, and financial results while examining the stated intentions of those seeking to privatize public education.

The current laws governing charters and vouchers have removed most of the responsibility and accountability for sound conservative financial practices from the charter industry with these words: "They receive public funding similarly to traditional schools. *However, they have more freedom over their budgets, staffing, curricula and other operations."*

This freedom has been used to profit by cutting staff benefits, hiring relatives, buying curricula from themselves, and self-dealing related party transactions for their operations.

The intent was to release charters from what was termed district "bureaucracies." A historical reference is due here. *Bureaucracies served monarchs, not democratically elected boards.* The use of the word, "bureaucracies," by Friedman and others, ignores the origin of the term. Bureaucrats served monarchs, not democratically elected boards. The use of this term belies the fact that the agent of those democratically elected boards is the superintendent as their agent he or she is subject to the will of those elected boards.

We have traded this democratically elected governance arrangement in for one where CEOs with related-party corporate boards have carte blanche to spend our tax-sourced funding at privately held charter schools.

In the mid-eighties, when districts began giving principals and teachers greater financial control over their schools, those newly freed employees were admonished with the following statement: "With great freedom comes great responsibility."

Site-based management, which gives teachers and principals control over their budgets, staffing, curricula, and other operations, has been the norm in school districts since the mid-1980s.

The bureaucracy arguments about districts were acted upon during the 1980s. What management model did we get by contracting out educational services?

Answer: oligarchies and monopolies.

"Bureaucracies" at school districts were replaced by contracted charter oligarchies and corporate monopolies with tens of thousands of backpacks full of cash paying for a contracted educational service with an educational management firm. This new model is supposed to pass as a financial innovation. Business efficiencies are supposed to be providing us with streamlined management of our schools based on business management principles. We tried this before.

SCIENTIFIC MANAGEMENT

Historically, when school systems adopted "business" efficiency methods, the results were catastrophic. Taylor's work *The Principles of Scientific*

Management was adopted by many school districts at the turn of the century. This was done during that era's stated desire to run schools as efficiently as the businesses of the time (Taylor, 1911).

Taylor's system was designed to "increase efficiency and save money." The old school desks[2] from this period are those bolted-down desk-and-chair combos that janitors would adjust to each child's height. This "innovation" saved a fortune on furniture. The effects on academic performance were marginal at best.

The rules of the game requiring school systems to bid for services and materials are there for a reason. When they weren't in place, graft and misappropriations of funds and deals with related parties and relatives were the norm. Trusting the market to correct this type of abuse does not work. Permissible and legal are two different things.

What has never been permissible or legal in district public schools is an overt cashing in on one's position of authority *at the expense of students*. This is not a claim that this type of behavior never occurs or has never occurred in districts. It has and does. That's why those pesky "regulations and policies" that privatizers disdain are there. It is also why the malaise in a real public school *is eventually caught, reported on, and punished*. It's called financial accountability.

Local political control of our public schools matters. It has been replaced by corporate control and a corporate culture.

NOTES

1. http://lpedia.org/1980_National_Platform#4._Education.
2. These type of desks and chairs are illustrated on the cover chosen for this book.

Chapter Twenty-One

A Corporate Culture

Educational service corporations are seeking to dominate the "educational marketplace." Educational (corporate) management organizations, EMOs or CMOs, are one manifestation of this type of corporate educational delivery system.

Market domination and expansion into new markets are how a free-market enterprise grows and thrives. However, growth is not always an indicator of sound business financials or academic prowess.

The mortgage markets in the United States were booming in the early part of this century. Those markets were growing exponentially. That financial bubble burst at great cost to the general public. The mortgage market was mainly financed with private investments; however, Fannie Mae and Freddie Mac contributed to the market failure with fast and loose lending parameters. The deregulation of the mortgage market by the federal government contributed to the bubble in real estate prices. The government's policies enabled the high-risk mortgage market by subsidizing risky mortgages.

Corporate culture can make the difference between sound economic growth based on solid debt-to-income ratios and overleveraged markets. The emerging charter financial markets appear to be acting with the same disregard for economically sound long-term debt-to-property ratios as the mortgage derivative market prior to 2007.

Federal and state tax-free bonds, a financial incentive to junk bond dealers financing the debt of the charter industry, are causing the market to overheat. The scale of this market is large enough to warrant concern over the effects of a debt-driven market crash in this sector on the overall economy.

There are currently 6,930 charter schools in forty-four states and the District of Columbia, serving just over three million of our children (Source: FY 2018 figures from Edreform).

The financial backers of the debt held by charter and private schools have been attracted to this marketplace by the size and scope of public education in this country. That marketplace accounted for $634 billion of expenditures in FY 2014. The economic theory driving the market makes clear that the educational "market" is about the *financial* markets, not the *educational* part of this phrase.

When the response is, "No, it's not about the money. It's about academic performance and accountability," *it denies the fact that the model is economic in nature.* The ruse is exposed when the businesses' CEOs declare their right to make as much money as they can, which is the truth.

When someone says, "It's not about the money," it's about the money.

—H. L. Mencken

The economic theory behind vouchers, private school scholarship tax credits, and charter schools is first and foremost about the money. Contracted services in privately held properties are substituted for community ownership of those assets and communal responsibility for educating our children.

The finances of this free market are not driven by educational principles. They are driven by bottom-line profits. Statements such as "It's not the money, it's the principle," are trumped by the financial data from this economic theory of action underlying this marketplace approach.

We are told that "charter schools are publicly funded, privately managed, and semi-autonomous schools of choice." "Publicly funded" refers to taxpayer funding from the state and federal governments and, in some states (outliers), access to the local communities' taxpayer resources. In most states with charters, these "public schools of choice" have access to tax-free bond funding. Other states have multiple ways[1] for charters to borrow tax-free bonds, with eleven states offering dedicated facilities funding to charter schools. An analysis of this distribution of funding sources, which was presented earlier, is restated here.

Twenty-three states allow charter school contractors to own the property and assets of the charter. In other words, they are able to sell the assets when they transfer ownership to another charter, or sell the property. In most cases,

Table 21.1. State Funding and Tax-Free Bond Support of Charter School Properties

State Dedicated Facilities Funding	State Grant Programs	Tax-Exempt Bonds	State Credit Enhancement	For Profits Allowed	Private Owner Allowed
11 States	13 States	33 States	6 States	21 States	23 States

transferring to a new charter contractor applies only to nonprofits. Charter holders are also able to assume debt on their property based on the properties' value *and the expected revenues from the state. That is, the students' "backpacks full" of cash are assets.*

Twenty-one states that have charter laws allow for-profit charter schools or charter management organizations. This is one less than half of the forty-four states with charter legislation in place. The privatized educational services market is consolidating as mega-charter groups take market share in limited geographical areas. There are also multi-state charter organizations with properties in several states and multinational charter corporations that have business interests in the United States educational market.

The charter industry cites charter student growth as proof that the free-market theories are validated by the data and that the market is sustainable. The data gathered over twenty-five years demonstrates that the new long-term debt and commitments authorized by bondholders use projections (estimates) of charter ADM growth as "collateral" (guarantees[2]) on the loans. In other words, the long-term loans are for amounts *greater than* the physical property and assets of the charter company.

Students and the Equalized Valuation Funding that follows them are counted as revenue in this equation.[3] *This makes sense until the estimates do not materialize.*

New construction is always a high-risk business venture, and the number of students one expects that building to attract seldom comes in as predicted. A company that is expanding needs to have the fiscal discipline to demonstrate a reserve of cash prior to an expansion. A solution may be to allow existing charters to borrow only up to the property's value and the existing revenue stream, a conservative fiscal approach to borrowing.

In Arizona, where charters continue to gain ADM (Average Daily Membership), this consolidation of the charter market has been made clear in four years of ADM growth data in the state. While ADM is increasing yearly at charters in Arizona and nationally, an analysis of the data on ADM growth in Arizona over the last four fiscal years conclusively *shows that the top ten charter companies captured 73.45 percent of the ADM increases.*[4] This pattern is apparent in other states as large charter groups outspend and outborrow the "competition."

The top five charter groups of that group of ten captured 60 percent of the charter market growth. The market is consolidating around these five major players. This pattern, as noted, is seen in other states with a history of charter expansion. There are examples of charter-holding companies that have 70-plus locations and tens of thousands of students in the national data, that is, "Success Academies." The Gulan Schools, operated under various names across the United States, control over 120 sites nationwide.

In Arizona, overall charter school ADM has grown by 29,549 full-time students from FY 2014 to FY 2017. Charter ADM growth currently represents 16 percent of all ADM in all public districts and charters combined. Most of that four-year gain in ADM was captured by the top ten (by ADM size) charter organizations (73.45 percent of all four-year ADM growth). Most of the remaining 417 charter organizations have either stagnated or have declining enrollment.[5]

In a prior chapter, this data was graphically presented on the total number of children in charter programs. The discussion here is on *the four-year gain in ADM*. When we look at the total number of students in charter schools, the top thirty charter companies in Arizona (out of 427 companies in FY 2017) controlled 63 percent of *total* charter ADM (133,244 students out of 179,255) at the end of Fiscal Year 2017. University-based charters controlled another 2,414.4 ADM. This small group's market share keeps growing as the market consolidates.

The remaining 380 charter companies shared a total of 64,009 ADM. But they captured only 5,434.56 new students when the university charters in the mix are deleted from the count. The data reflects the winners and losers in this

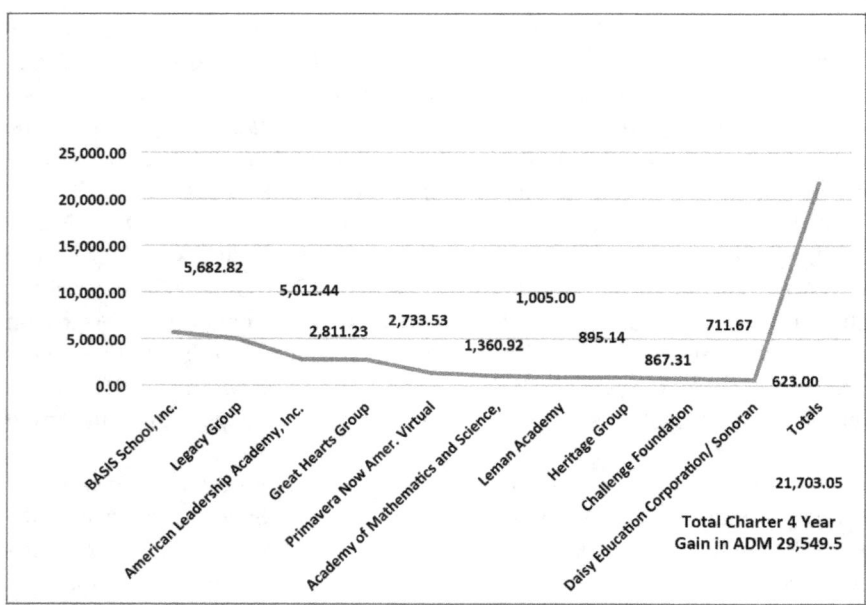

Figure 21.1. New ADM Distribution over Four Years (FY 2014 through FY 2017)
Source: Compiled ADM Data from FY 2014 to FY 2017 from Superintendent's Report with adjustments made for corrections to this report by the AZDOE in April of 2018

mix. Consolidation of the charter market is occurring, with fewer and fewer charter holders controlling more and more of the ADM.

This leaves the remaining charter holders, *whose long-term debt and lease commitments were premised on ever-increasing amounts of ADM,* in a financially untenable position. They cannot meet the debt loads on their lease-adjusted long-term debt.

Author's Note: University charters garnered 2,414.4 of the 7,846 ADMs shared by all other charters outside of the top ten (8 percent of the total four-year gain in ADM), leaving all other charter contractors with 5,434.6 of ADM growth to share (18.4 percent of the total four-year gain in ADM). Grand Canyon Institute's analysis benchmarked unsustainable ADM growth as a four-year growth rate that was less than 0.5 percent of current ADM.

The anticipated growth rate being used to justify long-term debt commitments typically called for a much greater rate of ADM growth (projections) on their loan documents. Stated rates in these audit documents called for double- and triple-digit ADM growth. When the numbers do not come in (as stated in the audit's listed plans to increase student numbers, such as increasing advertising and marketing), a net deficit occurs, that is, companies' liabilities exceed their assets. These are usually listed in the audits as a final note regarding Going Concern status.

GCI's tracking of ADM over five fiscal years indicates the numbers are not coming in (i.e., the growth plan didn't work). As noted earlier, the top thirty charter companies in Arizona (out of 427 in FY 2017) controlled 63 percent of all ADM (133,244 students out of 179,255 are in the top thirty charter groups).

Long-term debt is guaranteed by anticipated growth estimates of ADM. Committed lease payments are premised on ADM growing, not stagnating or decreasing.

The situation is exacerbated by the overleveraged position that these charter's properties are in (i.e., the charters that are losing ADM). This consolidation is typical in states that have had charters since the early 1990s. Market monopolies are developing. *These monopolies will eventually choke off academically performing charters that cannot compete with businesses that can enter the market with new facilities paid for with government-subsidized debt.*

A FINANCIAL HOUSE OF CARDS

Charter Corporations that use IDA bonds and charter capital company bonds borrow money based on, *and guaranteed by, projected future enrollment growth. This is why the IDA bonds are designated as "Educational Revenue*

Bonds." The loan amount[6] is linked to ADM growth, *not the actual market value of the properties.*

The datasets include cases in which the loans are leveraged at twice the actual market value of the properties and assets. Overall property values on Arizona charter contractors' properties are only 0.57 of the amount owed on those properties. The balance of the debt is guaranteed by expected revenues from the state on ADM.

To be clear, this means that the children's "backpacks full of cash" represent collateral for the loan.

When ADM growth fails to materialize, long-term leases and loan payments that were premised on student population growth create fixed expenditure requirements that exceed the charters' ability to pay their long-term lease-adjusted debt. This also occurs in cases in which the charter itself does not "own" the properties,[7] that is, in cases in which a subsidiary, related-party real estate company holds the debt and ownership of the property used to educate the students. Grants from the USDOE aid and abet this overextension of credit.

Federal funds from the USDOE to the states and individual charter holders use "Credit Enhancement for Charter School Facilities" grants to help charter owners gain access to the tax-free bond markets. These bonds are almost 100 percent held by the junk bond sector of the financial markets. These statements are not meant to be critical of the need for this type of financing. IDA bonds and credit enhancement tools have a function in the financing of charter debt. The issue is that the market has overleveraged that debt.

We are told, and charter contractors believe, that charter holders are the ones taking the financial risks on these properties. This financial risk is minimized by the way charters organize their businesses. Most charters are organized as LLCs or C Corps. This designation protects a business owner from many of the financial failure consequences associated with a business by limiting the owner's personal financial liability.

This business classification is typical in a "free market." It limits the business owner's financial risk and responsibility. Again, this is not a critique of this organizational practice. It is merely a statement about the personal risk being assumed by the charter holder.

Within the same time period, school districts in Arizona had $5.1 billion in debt on their properties and assets at the end of FY 2017. *The total depreciated value of those district properties was $20.7 billion. Property and assets were four times greater than the debt on those properties, with a property-to-debt ratio of 4 to 1.*

A Corporate Culture

The other side of the "competitive" educational market (charters) had different ratios going on. The data that follows starts by using the depreciated Property Values.

Relationship of Property Values to Debt Carried by Charters 0.715 to 1.

(Undepreciated Charter Property Value of $1.4 billion and its relationship to Long-Term Lease-Adjusted Debt Commitments of $2.56 Billion)

Discussion: Charters Property and Asset Debts Rely on Guaranteed Payments of ADM to back their IDA and other types of Long-Term debt. Long Term Leases are Commitments, that is, they must be paid. This relationship is referred to as Lease Adjusted Long Term Debt.

The second set of data reports depreciated Property Values, which is the same method used by the "competition," district schools. We did not include short-term debt or lines of credit in our calculations, a standard business financial practice when looking at debt issues. Inclusion of that debt would have conservatively added another $500 million to the debt load carried by charter contractors.

The level of under-water debt is on track to hit $1.5 billion for FY 2018 based on known refinancing activities during that fiscal year.

We, the public, are told that the charter business is responsible for this debt. We are also told that it is taking all of the financial risks. No matter how this risk is stated, there is a real loss of school buildings and assets when a charter defaults. When properties built as public school business sites are lost to repossession by debt holders, *there is a physical loss to the market in educational services.*

Preventing that type of loss should be a part of the mission of the authorizing agencies overseeing these "contracts." This mission is best served by

Table 21.2. Charter Shortfall on Debt and Commitments of $2.56 Billion

Long-Term Debt and Commitments at AZ Charters FY 2017: $2,563,792,686
FY 2017 Depreciated Value of Property and Assets of All Arizona Charter Properties $1,402,205,782
Relationship of Depreciated Property Value to Long-Term Debt and Lease Commitments 54.69% or .547 to 1
Shortfall in Dollars Property Value—Long-Term Debt and Commitments Using Depreciated Value −$1,161,586,904

Source: Consolidated Audit Data from FY 2016–2017

having district-elected boards oversee charter financial dealings within their communities,[8] that is, Dr. Ray Budde's original model.

Issuing contracts to a financially unstable educational service contractor is not a fiscally sound or conservative business practice.

If we use the road construction analogy, free-market businesses competing (bidding) in that market *need to show financial evidence that they will be able to deliver on the contract.* A feasibility study is done by the contracting state or municipality prior to awarding the contract.

Financial collapses during the school year represent a failure to deliver on the contract the charter has with the state. The funds paid to date should be recovered by the agency authorizing the contract (ASBCS) first, not debt holders. An undelivered service *was paid for using tax-sourced funds.*

This type of mid-school year failure has occurred eighty-two times since 1994. The money paid to the contractors who defaulted was not recovered.[9]

Charters that use commercial lending, as several in Arizona do, must meet the criteria set by a financial institution for their loans.[10] The charters that use these types of financing and leasing in the data appear to be financially sound.

Charter laws in two states limit the amount of debt charters can assume and require plans for eliminating even short-term debt. This is an example of sound fiscal regulation.

Commercial lending does not permit overleveraging of property and asset values. At a commercial business, it may also include inventory, accounts receivable, and other asset values. After the last mortgage crisis, one of the reinstated requirements for obtaining a residential mortgage was for buyers to bring a percentage of the property's value to the table when obtaining a mortgage.

Unless a normal commercial company is building in an area designated as a New Market Tax Credit zone, it cannot borrow tax-free bonds. School properties and hospitals are an added exception to the rules for New Market Tax Credit zones. These exceptions were added after charter laws were passed in early 2000 as a way to encourage investment in this market sector.

The reality is that most of the charter industry's bonds (77 percent)[11] are underwritten by IDA debt (tax-free bonds) held by junk bond investors. Junk bond grades of "CCC" (Extremely Speculative) are typical, with the highest-rated bonds listed at "Ba," which is considered Lower Medium Grade. The majority of IDA bonding is *unrated*, indicating that the firm the firm being bonded did not go through a financial rating process. Bonds that are unrated are traded as junk bonds.

Thirty-three states allow IDA bonds[12] to fund charter properties. *The bond amounts are not based on what the buildings and physical assets are worth in an open market. Those types of bonds (junk grade) incur multiple fees,*

Table 21.3. Non-Investment Grade Bond Ratings

Lower Medium Grade (somewhat speculative)	Ba	BB	BB
Low Grade (speculative)	B	B	B
Poor Quality (may default)	Caa	CCC	CCC
Most Speculative	Ca	CC	CC
No interest being paid or bankruptcy petition filed	C	C	
Lower Medium Grade (somewhat speculative)	Ba	BB	BB
In default	C	D	D

Source: Market Rating of Bonds by National Rating Agencies (Moody's, Standard and Poor's, and Fitch)

penalties for prepayments, and reserve requirements because of the high risk to the lender. We accommodated these types of costs in our assessment of charter debt.

We accommodated market growth and the charter's expansion into new market areas in our equations[13] on charter long-term debt. The bond markets' classification of this "tax-free" market as lower middle grade (speculative) and less confirms our analysis.

REAL ESTATE ACQUISITION COMPANIES

An analysis of the bond ratings in this sector indicated that a Ba was the highest bond rating listed in the market.[14] Typical were CCC bond ratings. CCC rated bonds are junk bonds. The largest amount of charter debt is "Unrated." Unrated bonds pay a higher interest rate and are considered junk grade. The result of "Credit Enhancements," tax-free bonds, and government loan programs is a market dominated by long-term debt held by the junk bonds industry. These bonds are bundled and traded like the mortgages bundled in the derivative markets prior to the last financial disaster in 2007.

Audit reviews indicate that a substantial number of charter properties in the data are "owned" by subsidiaries of the charter (in several cases, the charter is a subsidiary of the real estate holding company). These property-holding firms then "lease" the charter school properties back to their related party charter sites.

The leases often pay the holding company a premium on the lease.[15] The subsidiaries borrow the money for their loans using the charter's expected revenue from AZDOE as collateral (termed a "guarantee" on the audits). This is not an unusual business strategy (leasing from a subsidiary). GCI considered the debt held by the property holding firm and allowed for a 9 to 15 percent difference between debt payments and lease payments. This rate was considered a fair market return on investment risk.

EXACERBATING THE DEBT PROBLEM

The federal and state governments provide grant money to states to "enhance" charter credit (i.e., to make the owners eligible to borrow more than their assets would normally allow at a lower rate). This is not how "free markets" are supposed to work. The implied need for this type of credit enhancement is another tell about the financial precariousness of this "free" market. A solid financial investment does not need enhancing.

In the case of federal Charter Credit Enhancement grants, the federal government injects itself into the bond markets by enhancing the credit worthiness of charters that do not fit the "normal" parameters for financing the loans. Our financial markets have seen this type of credit enhancement before.

Fannie Mae and Freddie Mac held mortgages engaged in this type of speculative lending prior to the collapse of the mortgage markets in 2007. As if this were not enough, those mortgage markets were also underwritten by deliberately overrated financial derivatives.[16] Derivatives in that market had been given ratings that *were falsified by the rating agencies*. FINRA (the Financial Industry Regulatory Authority), the agency charged with regulating this market, has taken several charter bond dealers' licenses for misleading investors.[17]

These real estate–holding subsidiaries are not currently audited by the charter governing agency or the state's auditor general. If the company is a federal nonprofit, the data is available through the company's IRS 990 filing. *For-profit charter real estate firm's audits are not publicly available.* Only one state in the dataset requires the auditing of these subsidiary-related parties doing business as partner companies with the charter schools. This lack of reporting of related firms audits is a transparency issue.

Why would the Department of Education provide Charter Credit Enhancement funding?

The federal program's purpose for Charter Credit Enhancement grants is stated on the Department of Education's Office of Innovation and Improvement:[18] "The purpose of the Credit Enhancement program is to award grants to eligible entities that demonstrate innovative methods of helping charter schools address the cost of acquiring, constructing, and renovating facilities by enhancing the availability of loans and bond financing."

Thirty-three states have systems in place that allow charter owners to back their debt with "anticipated revenue" on anticipated ADM. That is, they are bonding their property and assets based on their students' anticipated backpacks full of cash. In Arizona, the long-term lease-adjusted debt per ADM is currently over $14,000. This is more than three times the amount of debt per ADM of districts. *The market in charter bonds is grossly overleveraged.*

LONG TERM LEASING COMMITMENTS WITH RELATED PARTIES

In charter states where a related company (subsidiary) is allowed to own the properties, the charter schools lease or rent their property from those subsidiary, related party, real estate companies.

These related party companies' *sole business income* is from leasing (or renting) charter sites to the charter school affiliated with the real estate holding company. The leases must be paid in order for the subsidiary to survive. If the leasing/real estate company is making a profit, which is the original business reason for setting up the subsidiary, that profit represents the variance between the loan payments and the lease commitment.

A typical variance was between 10 and 20 percent of the loan payments with built-in lease increments listed in the commitment sections of the audits. Several companies affiliated with Arizona charters' *main business* is the property holding arm of the enterprise, not education. These companies list the charters *as subsidiaries of those holding companies* on their audits. A fair Return on Investment (ROI) was determined to be between a 9 percent and 15 percent markup on the committed leases.

Note: Our datasets separated those real estate companies' $253 million of IDA debt out of our data calculations. This was to avoid double-counting of our lease adjusted long-term debt figures. Adjusting the data avoided double-counting the long-term lease payment charged by those companies to the charters with the long-term debt of the property-holding company. Great care was taken to avoid any duplication of the indebtedness measures, that is, long-term bond commitments, bond interest and finance charges, and long-term committed lease payments are undercounted.

In this model, the rules on property and asset ownership allow the business to count the student ADM as an "Asset" when the properties are bonded. Figure 21.1 illustrates a common leasing arrangement with a related party that holds the charters' real estate assets. Short-term debt in our datasets was handled in the same manner as Lines of Credit (LOC). That is, those amounts are not in the long-term debt *calculations. We handled and accounted for short-term debt differently than long-term debt as standard accounting practice calls for. This means our statistics are overly conservative.*

The sole source of income for these property management companies is the charter entities' long-term leases and rents they, the educational management

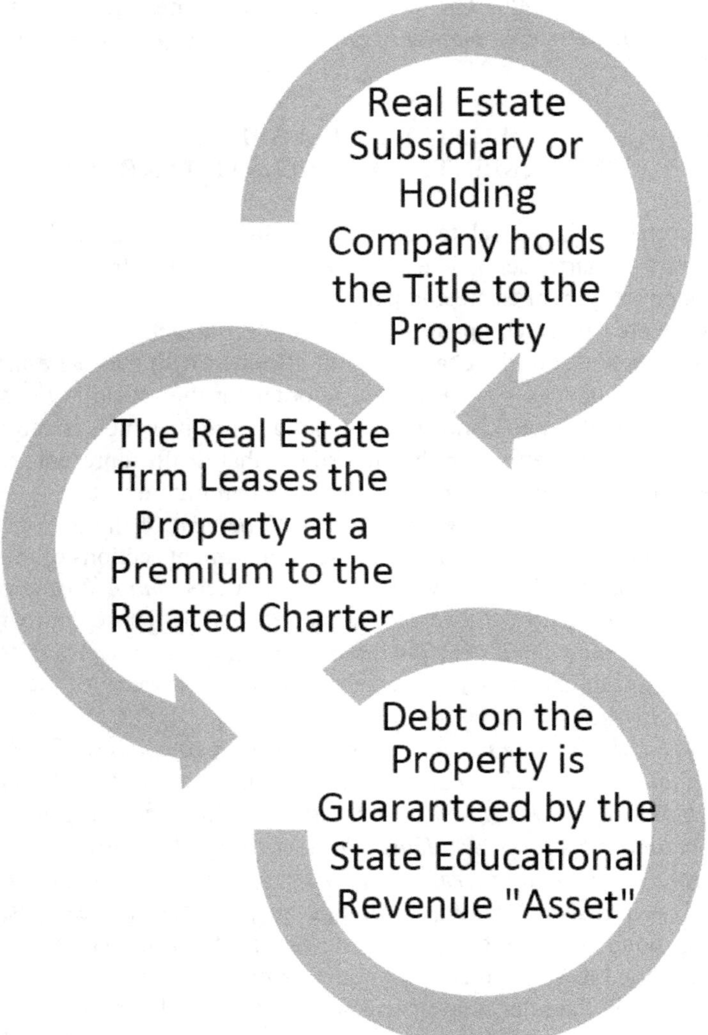

- Real Estate Subsidiary or Holding Company holds the Title to the Property
- The Real Estate firm Leases the Property at a Premium to the Related Charter
- Debt on the Property is Guaranteed by the State Educational Revenue "Asset"

Figure 12.2. A Real Estate Subsidiary's Relationship to the Charter School's Lease Commitment

organization or real estate subsidiary, rely on to meet their debt obligations on their bonds. Charters are also allowed to collect donations and, in Arizona, are eligible for tax credit donations from parents and businesses.

We include donations made with tax credits to the donor as part of this analysis, as they are listed in audit revenues. In summary, the only way the property-holding business can earn a profit is to charge more for the lease than the long-term bonds are costing the real estate holding subsidiary that "owns" the properties in question.

Long-term lease commitments are prevalent in the data and binding in cases where the property is held by a related party or affiliated corporate real estate holding subsidiary of the charter. Loans (bonds) on the property are guaranteed by educational revenues coming in for the students at the charter. No matter which company actually holds the bond debt, the source of the funds paying that debt is educational revenue paid out by the state.

Leasing properties to franchisees or subsidiaries is a common business model. McDonald's owns most of the real estate holdings and any debt associated with those buildings and uses long-term leases with its franchisees. However, unlike the charter market, McDonald's is not being paid with taxpayer funds and is not subsidizing its real estate portfolio with tax-free bonds.

UNDER-WATER REAL ESTATE HOLDINGS

When debt or lease payments are not based on property value but on an anticipated income stream (from ADM growth on the "asset" represented by students), liabilities can, *and in most cases do,* exceed the real property assets' market value.

The data indicates a charter real estate marketplace that is overleveraged with properties that are "under water" (to use a term from the last mortgage crisis). In this case, *under water* means the property is not worth the amount owed on the debt and commitments *and the charter's ADM is not materializing as expected.*[19]

There will be a predicted $1.5 billion shortfall between charter property and asset values at Arizona charters and their long-term debt and commitments in FY 2018. The figure is offset by those charters with a positive balance between long-term debt and their properties' values. This figure does not include another $0.5 billion of short-term debt and lines of credit or commitments to related party leased employee contracts, service contracts, and equipment leases.

All of which must be paid.

OVERLEVERAGED LONG-TERM DEBT AND COMMITMENTS

Like the mortgage crisis in 2007 and 2008, this situation has been developing over a period of time. Overleveraged bonds and loans generate excessive debt and interest payments, which, in turn, create negative net assets (Net Deficits).[20] Refinancing to reduce debt interest payments *is a short-term solution* (and often costly due to built-in prepayment penalties), but can be detrimental when used as a long-term solution.[21]

This finding regarding charter bonds is in contrast to findings in a 2014 report on charter debt (performed by the bond industry). That report *did not fully consider the effects of refinancing*[22] (Marek 2014). It also *did not perform an analysis on the risks of continuous remortgaging on properties that were under water.* As an historical reference, the bond ratings of derivative products sold during the 2007–2008 mortgage crisis were also highly rated by the rating agencies. The ratings of those derivatives, as we found out, were "untruthful."

Homeowners who are still under water on their mortgages are still paying for that free market's solution set. Government money was used in that market meltdown to bail out the free-market financial groups and overextended companies.

We believe that the Department of Education's grants for enhancing charters' credit rating doubles down on the risk to our taxpayer-funded private contractors' property and debt. We have seen the results of this type of financial manipulation before. As the extent of the last financial meltdown became apparent, the public rightfully asked, "How could this have happened?"

Answer: We trusted free-market economics to self-correct. They didn't. Only truly free, free markets do have a chance of self-correcting. In those types of free markets, the bond investors are really the ones taking the capital risks along with the business owners and shareholders.

The subsidized and publicly financed nature of this market (charters) make it neither a free nor a true capitalistic model. The market is committing what Friedman himself termed as "business suicide." By seeking government subsidies and financial exemptions, the consequences will not only affect the charter market. The losses will also be consequential to public funding, as the market experiments "indirectly" with their tax dollars.

Who is holding all of this high-risk, high-profit debt? When a deeper analysis is performed, one comes up with a list of bond-holding firms that is reminiscent of the companies behind the last mortgage crisis and the junk bond fiascos[23] in the last century. Junk bond dealers bundle the securities in their portfolios and sell them to fund managers.

Charter bonds are often "bundled" in the bond markets in a manner similar to the bundling of mortgages during the last decade.[24] In that overextended market, several bond rating companies were cited for their rating of mortgage bonds' grades.

Another factor leading to the last crash was the use of derivatives in the overheated mortgage market. Several charter companies in our analysis guaranteed the total of a bundled group's debt by banding five charter companies together as a group. A default by one hurt all of the other charters in the group as they were still all responsible for the debt. A chain reaction of closures followed.

This type of financial manipulation and high-risk behavior is what has happened consistently in our historic experiences with deregulated financial industries.

NOTES

1. The fact that some states have multiple ways for charters to finance their property means that this table will not equal the number of charter states.
2. Guaranteed loans based on anticipated revenues are transferred directly from the Department of Education to the debt holder. That is, the charter holder does not receive the cash first. This negates the flexibility and autonomy of the owner to innovate, especially when long-term debt is a major portion of the charter's portfolio. We believe children are not commodities.
3. The term "backpacks full of cash" was coined to describe this funding following the student to their school of choice.
4. ADM Counts are on the *Annual Superintendent's Report*, the source used for this analysis. For the first time, ADM growth at charters exceeded ADM growth at district schools (FY 2017) in Arizona.
5. An ADM growth rate of under .5 percent over four years was considered stagnated growth in our equations.
6. Several short-term loans analyzed were also based on anticipated ADM for the following year. These loans were typically a stopgap measure to provide cash flow to the company.
7. Another factor: AZDOE often "overpays" charters, especially online schools, based on their reported projections and counts. In FY 2014 charters collected $26 million this way (overpayments). This money is then systematically reclaimed by AZDOE in the following year's Equalized Funding Payment by withholding funds the following fiscal years.
8. Capacity at existing charters was measured in GCI's first report, "Following the Money." Charter student capacity is currently greater than the actual number of students attending charter schools. On the positive side, in Arizona, the building of charter schools helped solve a facilities shortage when the state's population grew exponentially in the late twentieth century and continues to grow at an extremely fast pace in this century.
9. Another issue is online schools being paid for undelivered services. In FY 2014, over $26 million was overpaid to online schools. The companies have a portion of this recurring error withheld from the next year's Equalized Valuation Payments: an unending zero interest loan.

10. For example, Northland Preparatory in Arizona has a 3 percent loan from Chase Bank. This company also has a representative corporate board, an exemplar in the Arizona charter market.

11. Source: Collation of Audit Data on Long-Term Debt, Holders of the Debt, and Interest Rates for FY 2017. Analysis was also performed on FY 2014 through 2017.

12. For a discussion of New Market Tax Credits, see *Carpetbagging America's Public Schools* or https://www.cdfifund.gov/programs-training/Programs/new-markets-tax-credit/Pages/default.aspx. Credit enhancement grants from states and the federal government can impact the rate a charter is charged for its bonds. They are another form of government interference in what is supposed to be a "free market."

13. For a detailed report on charter debt in Arizona, see: www.grandcanyoninstitute.org paper, *Red Flags: Overleveraged Debt* published in January 2019.

14. An outlier of AAA was found in the data. However this was an IDA loan that was being paid for by a lease from a district (Higley, AZ). Thus the higher rating and a reflection on the credit worthiness of districts in Arizona.

15. A normal multileveled business practice in the free-market model.

16. Editors, 2015; Fabricant, 2012; Green, 2017; Green, Preston, and Baker, 2016.

17. See: https://www.finra.org/sites/default/files/Lawson_Complaint_051916_2.pdf.

18. https://innovation.ed.gov/what-we-do/charter-schools/credit-enhancement-for-charter-school-facilities-program/.
Arizona Legislation on this type of enhancement program for public and charter schools is located at: https://www.azleg.gov/ars/15/02155.htm.

19. In our analysis GCI considered ADM growth of .5 percent or less over four years as unsustainable (i.e., a net loss of ADM). This is a very conservative number as most of the cases predicted double-digit ADM growth in their projections.

20. Negative net assets are written as net (deficits) on financial statements with a bracket to indicate the negative amount. This paper and the supporting datasets use this convention and red coloring when there are net (deficits) indicated.

21. Relying on Junk Bonds to finance underwater properties backed by credit enhancements has a negative fiscal history. It is no wonder that the involvement of the Milken brothers and their partners in charter schools and earlier in daycare centers is verified in the data. This involvement is a troubling sign of who is profiting from these type of transactions and charter schools nationally. See https://www.investopedia.com/terms/m/michaelmilken.asp. Portable Practical Education, which is K–12, is one of the largest groups in Arizona. Equally disturbing is the money from real estate acquisition and imported (using work visas) teachers in the Gulen Schools identified in the data. This company's travel budget reflects travel costs that exceed $1M.

22. The report just focused on the data that showed the old debt paid. It negated the fact that this repayment was tied to refinancing a *greater* amount of debt.

23. The Milken brothers were the original holders of the charter group known as K–12 Inc. Mike Milken was known as "the Junk Bond King." He is no longer able to deal in the bond markets.

24. Commercial investors are sometimes unaware of the way these bundled debt packages are being sold. For example, the California Teachers Retirement fund is vested in K–12 Inc. stock. In the last market bubble burst, several teachers' retirement funds were burned by this type of investment. K–12 is a Milliken, the junk bond king, owned company.

Chapter Twenty-Two

Is This Any Way to Run a Business?

On June 25, 2018, the *Arizona Republic* reported on the State of Arizona's impending takeover of the Murphy School District. School districts in Arizona, as in the rest of the union, are not allowed to overspend their budgets.[1] Districts must comply with standard business accounting principles known as GAAP (Generally Accepted Accounting Principles). The reason for these regulations is that they protect the taxpayers' investments in public education. They are a safeguard ensuring the district does not overspend its authorization.

DOUBLE STANDARDS FOR FISCAL ACCOUNTABILITY

During the same fiscal year, 2017–2018, several charter schools shuttered their doors, closing suddenly and without warning to parents or students due to financial issues. In the Grand Canyon Institute report entitled "Red Flags: Net Losses and Net Assets (Deficits)," Grand Canyon Institute demonstrated that greater scrutiny of the Net Losses and Net (Deficits) by the Arizona State Board for Charter Schools might have prevented these sudden closures during an ongoing school year. That is, the closure should have occurred at the end of the prior school year.

Timely intervention would have allowed the closure to occur either at the end of the year or prior to the next school year. The current financial accountability system does not provide a check on whether the company being contracted with can deliver the contracted service the state is funding.

There is currently a double standard when it comes to accounting for the money spent at charter contracting firms and the similarly sourced funding at the "competition" districts. This educational market sector, charter and vouchered contracted services, has been deregulated. As a result of this deregulation, charters don't have to follow the financial rules that districts do. *The issue is that as private businesses operating in a publicly funded marketplace, they do not appear to be following standard business financial standards.*

The "competition" to local districts and schools is free to overextend itself and build new sites right next to aging district schools abiding by the "rules." If this were an athletic competition, this double standard would be the equivalent of one side being allowed to use performance-enhancing drugs while the other is being tested continuously to ensure that they are disqualified if they do the same thing.

The legislature responded quickly to an ethics violation at the Scottsdale School District when the superintendent used a related party to fulfill a contract.

It is telling that, when given the chance to add the same "restrictions" on related party transactions and gifts to charters, the same legislature demurred. Related party transactions remain sacrosanct at charters. *Legislators with an interest in charters voted in favor of greater restrictions on district-related party transactions while keeping the same transactions at charters legal.*

The reason given: Charters are private businesses.

THERE ARE NO FAIL-SAFES BUILT INTO THE MODEL

When net losses occur at districts, there is a mechanism in public school finance rules to prevent those losses from becoming catastrophic financial failures. The records in multiple years of ASBCS (Arizona State Board for Charter Schools) audits show that net losses[2] at charter sites have grown from 122 sites in FY 2014 to 162 sites in FY 2017. *These figures do not reflect all of the charter sites with net losses, because, to be conservative, the data analysis only consider those losses that were greater than $100K.* Our final analysis also considered other factors in order to ensure we did not label a charter that was growing as financially stressed. This required the researchers to define and set a standard for unsustainable losses. In other words, we identified the financial tells in an expanding market's data indicative of pending collapse.

DEFINING UNSUSTAINABLE LOSSES IN A GROWING "FREE MARKET"

Million-dollar-plus net losses affected 106 charter sites of Arizona charter sites in FY 2017. In our public policy reports, we demonstrated that a rate of financial loss greater than –$500 per ADM (Average Daily Membership) is unsustainable. For example, if a company has 200 full ADMs and is losing –$500 per ADM, it is losing $100,000 per year. The total net loss at this company is unsustainable. Another company with 1000 ADM *can* sustain the $100K level of net loss because the loss is only –$100 per ADM. While it is still a loss, the increases the school can expect in ADM can be expected to eventually stabilize the company's debt.

These *overly prudent cut point figures accommodate charters that are expanding their businesses.*[3] The researchers also sought to show that Net (Deficits) that exceed –$400 per ADM are long-term indicators of unsustainable losses. The data here shows total net losses at all charter sites over four years. These figures are given to show the growth in net losses over those four years.

We suggest the following: If you are claiming you are a business, account like a business.

If you are running your schools "like a business," it behooves your organization and the oversight agencies charged with monitoring your businesses to use standard business financial standards, that is, debt-to-income standards, business credit standards regarding debt to asset values, and generally accepted, account-detailed, audit reporting.

Any state tax-funded expenditures *should be having a positive effect on the local and state economies.* Charters that are sending money to out-of-state related parties are moving those services to another state and, as is the case in several charters, to another country.

The current deregulated use of state tax-sourced funding is also moving money and capital from locally collected (i.e., from the citizens in those communities) state tax funding out of the local economy.

One of the largest businesses and employers in the local community is public schools. The money being lost to the community when those educational services are contracted out is not being spent on the local businesses that chambers of commerce are supposed to represent. Chambers of commerce that support the current charter laws need to rethink the economics of that decision.

The deregulation of public school financing has created an opportunity for charter schools to apply "business models" that ensure the business maximizes its profits without serious financial, political, or social accountability. The same lack of accountability allows the market to operate without regard to financial rules of thumb regarding debt-to-income related party transactions, nepotism, and debt-to-property considerations.

Milton Friedman would say this is the purpose of a business, to make a profit (Friedman, 1982; Friedman, 1990). The issue isn't about whether a profit can or should be made. Deregulation has granted the charter industry *absolute power* over how individual charter contractors spend the taxpayer-sourced resources the organizations receive for contracted services with the state.

Great financial freedom has been granted with limited accountability for the responsible use of those publicly sourced funds. Educational funds are supposed to be going toward the education of our future citizens.

This work does not take issue with a business making a profit. It does take exception to the idea that businesses operating with taxpayer funding can ignore sound financial standards and practices. Twenty-three percent of the market does so using a business model that has a social responsibility built into it. Good for them.

A conservative financial philosophy regarding the expenditure of taxpayer funds takes the last part of Friedman's thesis to heart: "There is one and only one social responsibility of a business, that is to use its resources and engage in activities designed to increase its profits *so long as it stays within the rules of the game, which is to say, engages in open and free competition without deception or fraud.*"

The current "rules of the game" are purposefully designed to *be too weak to ensure* this market is open and free without deception and fraud.

The rules of the game have been deregulated. The body overseeing the market (the state charter board) does not have the fiscal authority to step in prior to a financial collapse.[4] Business suicide is occurring in this market as a result of exceptions to the rules that were lobbied for by the industry. This market sector has succeeded in placing into charter laws government-paid subsidies and tax-free bonds.

In a later paper, Dr. Friedman warned about what he called "business suicide" (Friedman, 1999). Business suicide happens when a business seeks exceptions and supports from the government to enable their efforts to capture additional funding or a favored status from the government.

As with any situation involving power, whether it is political or economic, "power corrupts and absolute power corrupts absolutely." In the meantime, the communities' efforts to maintain its public school structure are being shortchanged. Financial capital losses in a community directly impact economic, political, and social capital in that community.

We have argued that the current structure is giving charter-holder businesses too much government-sponsored and financed leeway through *tax-free junk bonds*[5] (a form of government subsidizing of the "free market"). State and federal grants aid and abet this so-called charter-free market. A state-sanctioned removal of regulations designed to ensure the standard financial practices codified in public school finance policies ensures there is limited public oversight when the contractors are spending publicly generated funds.

Credit enhancements from the USDOE and state governments exasperate the overextended, overleveraged market. *Bad debt with a lower interest rate is still bad debt.* Our research on the market's financial stability have conservatively demonstrated that an overleveraged bond market that counts on educational revenues as part of the collateral on the loans heightens the danger of a financial collapse. This collapse is occurring now in the publicly financed privately-held charter and voucher marketplace.[6]

We have failed to trust but verify.

Figure 22.1 illustrates the chain of possession by showing how the tax revenues flow from the state. An "intercept" sends the funds owed on debt directly to the junk bond debt holder and the remainder on to the charter contractor.

The "backpacks full of cash" are legally allowed to be intercepted. The reason for this is that those backpacks full of cash, which represent the state's Equalized Funding revenues and additional funding for purchasing and maintaining property ($2,000 per ADM), were used to guarantee payments on the contractor's privately held property and assets. *Assets* in this case include the charter's expected revenue from ADM revenue *as the main asset for the guarantee on the property and assets.*

How is this all possible? It's not what we were told.

Recall the National Conference of State Legislatures'[7] latest definition of charters: "They are privately managed by an organization that has a charter, or contract, with an authorizer." Following the money in the diagram shows that *part of the revenues meant to pay for the contractor's contract with the state is going to the debt holders first*, sometimes up to 20 percent of all funding. The chain of possession of money that the taxpayers paid the state to educate our children goes to the "intercepting" bondholders before the "contractor" takes possession of the balance from the state.

State Funding for Student ADM: Taxpayer Funds from State DOE due as contractual payments to educational contractors (charter holders).

Bond Holders intercept their bond payments directly from State Department of Education disbursements to the charter to pay bond holder "guaranteed" debt first. Reason: Educational Revenue Estimates on ADM were used to "Guarantee" the bonds.

Balance of contracted educational services fees from the state are then distributed in payments to the Charter contractor to provide Educational Services.

Figure 22.1. Flow of Tax Funding to Debt Holder Then to Contractor
Source: Reporting on Guarantees of Debt and Intercepts of Funding from Audits: FY 2014 through FY 2017

The state is de facto a collection agency for the bondholders. The state dutifully sends monthly payments to those debt holders *first* with the balance sent onward to the actual contractor being paid to provide an education. This transfer occurs prior to the delivery of any educational "service" that funding was authorized to pay.

The greater the guaranteed debt, the greater the intercept. The greater the intercept, *the less money that makes it to the contractor to actually provide educational services. Debt is paid first, subcontracted management costs second, educational services delivery a distant third. In a financial collapse, the first to go is the delivery of educational services as the school closes its doors.*

THEORETICAL SAFEGUARD

An economic free market is theorized to correct itself. "Market corrections" are supposed to assure the public that market driven academic and financial accountability in a free market will weed out financial misbehavior. The theory is that the decision making implied in parents' freedom to choose will result in parents removing their children from academically underperforming charter schools. That choice by a critical mass of parents will self-correct the market. This theory was first debunked by Fuller in 1997 (Fuller 1997).

This "exit" theory fiscal correction of an educational market based on academic performance is not supported in the research on why people exit from an organization (Hirschman, 1970), that is, it's not really how people choose. Hirschman's work in *Exit, Voice and Loyalty* is also confirmed by the seminal work on charter schools and vouchers, *Who Chooses, Who Loses*, a work that looked at the realities of why parents choose schools for their children. The theory is further questioned by Hoxby's *Reforms for Who?* (Fuller, 1997; Hoxby, 2003).

At present, the financial information about the contracted service provider is not sufficiently clear. Consumers of educational services do not have the financial data needed to allow them to choose based on whether or not the company may financially survive another year. Our analysis of twenty-four years of data on closures in Arizona showed eighty-two (19.2 percent) of the charter site closings in the state took place *during the school year*. The parents had no idea these closings were imminent. They did not have the political capital needed to demand financial information from the service provider they chose. At a minimum, this type of financial information needs to be available to parents if the goal is to provide a *viable and deliverable* choice.

This work challenges the assertion that "a free market will self-correct"[8] using the financial data from FY 2014 through FY 2017. We now have over twenty-four years of data. The marketplace's historical data results contradict the theoretical economic predictions (Bulkley, 2002; Chingos, 2014; Consoletti, 2011; Davenport, 2013; Editors, 2015).

THREATENED EDUCATIONAL CAPITAL SOURCES

The data in our studies and other scholarly reports points to a market that is neither free nor open. The market is also financially unstable. This situation is affecting and *threatening both financially stable, academically performing charter companies, communities, and district public school sources of revenue (public funds). In other words, the communities' educational economic capital is threatened.*

The efforts to deregulate and replace our public schools with free-market contractors and private schools have been enabled by legislation[9] created at the state and federal level to bypass locally enacted district policies regarding how public funds can be spent. These rules allow charter contractors the "freedom" to use their property and assets to guarantee the company's long-term debt. These rules also authorized the use of related party subsidiary firms and related party transactions with those firms. *Political control at charters is vested in corporate boards and CEOs, not an elected board.*

This combination of factors leads to financially compromised insider deals.

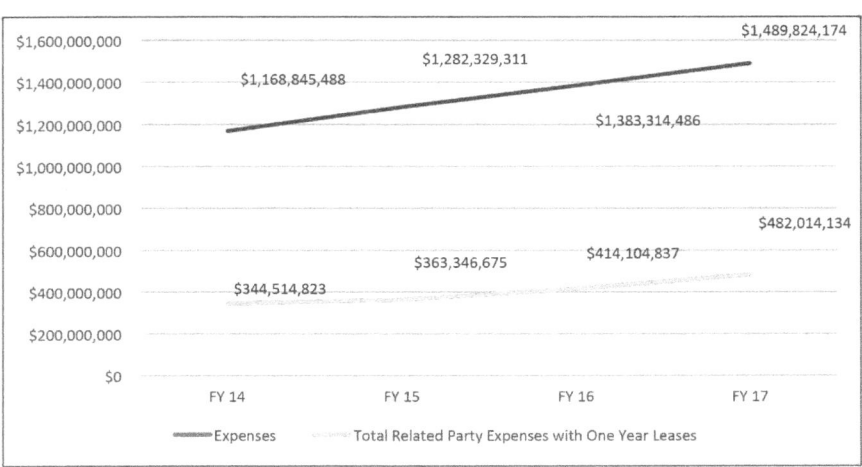

Figure 22.2. Charter Expenses Compared to All Related Party Expenses for Four Years
Source: Collated FY 2014–FY 2017 Related Party Expenses from Audits and IRS Form 990s

Crony capitalism, not free-market capitalism, is the result. Oligarchies where a single family controls the company have created monopolies. A faux form of capitalism has emerged where the source of the capital and the funding of debt are tax revenues and tax-free junk bonds, not private investments based on sound financial lending. This is evident in the totals (greater than 50 percent of expenditures) being spent on related party expenses as they relate to the charter industries total expense outlays.

BACKPACKS FULL OF DEBT GUARANTEED BY STUDENTS' BACKPACKS FULL OF CASH

The expression "backpacks full of cash" has been used to describe taxpayer funding following children to their school of choice. We contend that backpacks full of debt on properties the public does not own are a "clear and present danger" to our educational funding sources. If steps are not taken to stem the burgeoning debt in the charter sector, these payments will consume more and more of the dollars being spent to educate our future citizens.

Financially triggered charter closures are accelerating, not declining. In Arizona, this is occurring despite ever-increasing extra payments for charters to pay their leases and mortgages (currently, over $2,000 per student). The

Figure 22.3. Graphic Cartoon: Backpacks Full of Debt

taxpayers are funding this "extra payment," which is allowing the contractors to obtain additional privately held capital assets.

This additional funding is further exacerbating the problem by allowing even greater leveraging of debt. The evidence is that when these payments go up, the levels of debt are also increasing at a greater rate than the value represented by property and assets.

We contend that backpacks full of debt on properties the public does not own are a "clear and present danger" to our educational funding sources.

The "backpacks full of cash" following our students have degenerated into "backpacks full of debt" tied to the public's capital investments in public education. Private firms have accumulated debt and commitment levels that would not be tolerated in districts by the governing boards overseeing them. The public has lost its political capital and the economic capital associated with public education spending as a result of the state's contracting of educational services to private contractors. Legislation has exempted these businesses from the rules of the game for districts *and the financial rules normal businesses operate under.*

True free-market businesses do not rely on taxpayer funding or tax-free loans for their capital investments. Those now-deregulated rules protected taxpayers' capital acquisition funding and prevented districts from taking on more debt than the taxpayers can pay. The cost?

An estimated $400 million+ of Arizona charter contractor's property and assets have been lost to creditors since 1994. If a conservative multiplier of 10 is used to estimate the losses nationwide, the figure rises to $4 billion. A significant loss of educational and financial capital.

As of June 2017, a total of 27 percent of charter sites did not meet the Arizona State Board for Charter School's own financial performance expectations. This is an improvement over the statistics for Fiscal Year 2013–2014, which showed that one-third of charter organizations did not meet the financial performance expectations established by the ASBCS. However, the category *"Going Concerns" (an ASBCS red mark on the Financial Performance Expectations)* grew and was present on seventy-seven charter sites' financial scores (13.65 percent of all 576 sites). *Just under 20 percent of all charter sites lost more than $500 per student in FY 2017. Losing over $500 per student constitutes an unsustainable loss.*

We have drawn data from the ASBCS' audits and Financial Performance Expectation reports as primary sources. The audits were then cross-checked using Annual Financial Reviews (AFRs) at AZDOE and IRS 990 reports gleaned from Guide Star. We then consolidated the data by charter groups similar to the way some large charters post their consolidated audits to ASBCS.

Table 22.1. New ADM Distribution over Four Years (FY 2014 through FY 2017)

% ADM Overall Gain at the Top 10 Charter Companies:	73.45%
ADM Numerical Gain Posted by Top Ten:	21,703
ADM Gain Shared by Remainder (417 Charter Corporations):	7,846
Total Numerical Gain of ADM FY 14 to FY 17 ALL CHARTERS	29,549

Source: Compiled ADM Data from FY 2014 to FY 2017 from Superintendent's Report with adjustments made for corrections to this report by the AZDOE in April 2018

The next table illustrates the ASBCS's own assessment regarding how charters are faring on the financial expectations outlined by the ASBCS. For the first time, this board has the authority to close charters based on financial performance (as of June 2018). This system of checks and balances still needs work, but the AZ Charter Board's work is a positive step in the right direction.

NOTES

1. There is a mechanism available to districts that requires a special vote: a budget override. In many northeastern states, there are budget committees that must approve school district spending.

2. Conservative Data: GCI *did not* include Net Losses of less than $100K in its analysis. A total of fifty-nine additional sites had Net Losses that were less than $100K. These are not included in these tables or on the graphs shown in this work. This is a deliberate undercounting because such losses at a small charter (ADM < 100) are unsustainable.

3. We will also be questioning the use of IDA tax-free junk bonds and the method used to rate and justify the amounts on those bonds.

4. In May 2018, the ASBCS was given the ability to act when a charter does not meet their Financial Performance Recommendations. The board is currently rethinking their financial performance criteria, a much-needed change. To their credit, the ASBCS sought this change out.

5. There is a place for this type of bonding. We are arguing that the current lack of oversight of the market, including not placing limits on the number of charter schools in a community, is destroying academically performing charters and districts.

6. GCI understands that business finances are different from district finances in substantive ways. Districts are defined by the geographical area in which they are located. What advantage charter businesses have is that they can be in multiple locations AND use consolidated financials to support their charter network. The chief investigator managed districts, district charters, and Arizona charters. This experience is backed by practical experience running non-school businesses and an organization and management master's degree, mathematics, and financing expertise. He also

lectured to graduate and doctoral classes on identifying financial indicators in audits and required financial filings.

7. http://www.ncsl.org/research/education/charter-schools-overview.aspx.

8. The idea that the only purpose of a business is to make a profit has been challenged in the financial literature as economists have the hindsight of the last mortgage meltdown, the junk bond failures in the last century, and the demise of the Savings and Loans industry in their collective memory. See: https://www.forbes.com/sites/stevedenning/2013/06/26/the-origin-of-the-worlds-dumbest-idea-milton-friedman/#543b9e2d870e.

9. There are multiple cases of state representatives and state senators cashing in on the vague financial laws and rules that they voted on. Normal conflicts of interest have been made legitimate by legislating charter laws that permit activities the public would associate with a conflict of interest in a true public school.

Chapter Twenty-Three

Lost Political Capital

Public political life in this republic once followed a path that went like this: school board member, town council or selectman, state representative, state senator, U.S. Representative, and then U.S. Senator. In several New England states, vestiges of pure democratic processes still persist. Residents still gather yearly in their community to approve their schools' budgets and express their views on the direction of public education in those communities. The same citizens gather again to approve their town budgets and select local leadership.

Politicians used to prove their commitment to their community and country by military service or community activism on public boards and then a move upward to state and federal offices. This ensured that those moving on to national offices were in touch with and knew the communities they represented.

We have forgotten our civics lessons[1] and the wisdom of Tip O'Neill when he said, "All politics is local." A recent *New York Times* power post noted that, "In the age of President Trump, surging seas of activists on the left and the right are drowning out local issues and forcing senators and representatives to answer locally for every national controversy. Never has that new environment been so perfectly captured than over the past week, when lawmakers returned home to their congressional districts. They discovered, if they didn't know already, that most voters *were no longer paying much attention to core issues in their own communities*." (Note: This author does not blame Mr. Trump for this shift. It predates the current president and involves all of the political parties.) Civic engagement at the local level is waning at the same time it should be growing. As Pogo[2] noted, "We have met the enemy, and it is us."

We ignore the condition of our community's educational systems at our own peril. *Contracting out to multinational, regional, and statewide charter corporations removes control of public education out of the community and into the corporate boardroom.*

A publicly owned and locally governed comprehensive public school system is currently the only set of school choices in the marketplace where the physical assets *always* belong to the public. They are also the only choice where the enterprise of education is governed by a democratically elected board.

When reviewing the lists of failed charter high schools and elementary schools, one begins to contemplate that each represents a physical location that the "graduates" can no longer return to as alumni. The social capital of having a place called your town's public school is lost, and the replacement has a 50 percent chance of not being there after ten years. The capital losses to the community are economic, political, and social.

Public schools are and always have been designed to enable all citizens of the republic to receive a common educational experience tied to their community. The goal has always been to produce community-connected citizens of a democratic republic. When the Arizona-based Granite Hot Shot team lost their lives in the tragic Yarnell Fire, the community and relatives gathered at the local junior high school. This type of gathering place that belongs to the citizens of a community is there when tragedy or an emergency shelter is needed because the community owns this center of their community life. We take this availability of public spaces for granted.

While the "Neighborhood Effect" was an economist's justification for using public funding for privately held schools, the antithesis of what makes a neighborhood school special is one of the "unintended" consequence of "school choice." On this road to perdition, the first legislative step was to declare "open enrollment" at our community schools, a deliberate step designed to detach community schools from their community.

Table 23.1. Charter ADM Relationships to Revenue, Assets, and Debt

	2015–2016	2016–2017
Total ADM of Counted Sites	160259.68	172691.24
All Audit Revenues of Counted Sites	$1,433,505,294	$1,507,632,312
Depreciated Asset Value Counted Sites	$1,319,068,429	$1,402,205,782
Assets to ADM	$8,230.82	$8,119.73
Long-Term Debt Lease Adjusted Debt at Counted Sites	$2,364,443,629	$2,563,792,686
Long-Term Lease Adjusted Debt per ADM	$14,753.83	$14,846.11
Shortfall in Dollars at Counted Sites	$(1,045,375,200)	$(1,161,586,904)
Shortfall per ADM of UNDERWATER DEBT	$(6,523)	$(6,726)

This was sold as a way to provide parents with a choice that wasn't based on where you lived. The "backpacks of cash" did not follow the students going to an inter-district "choice." That funding did follow children moving to a charter school. How is that fair to the local taxpayers?

On top of that, we are not getting value for our contracted educational dollars.

Brand-new charters spring up in districts with aging facilities and *next to other performing charter* schools that have foregone risky financing. The shiny new charters are financed by state largesse and extra funding that more than covers the bond payments and interest.

Adding insult to injury, the new school may be owned by a company that did not pass the limited financial expectations of the charter board. This travesty is passed off as competition in a "free market." Four of the last five charter failures (closed during the school year) in Arizona fit the financing model being discussed here.

How *should* debt to revenue figures look?

As a contrast, the district figures on the same measures are also provided for two years: FY 2016 and FY 2017.

Adding insult to injury again, the federal government colludes with this privatization model. Rules regarding the role of the federal government in local education have been discarded.

Table 23.2. Arizona District's ADM Relationships to Revenue, Assets, and Debt

Fiscal Year	2015–2016	2016–2017
Total ADM all District Schools in Arizona	930877.255	1110353.445
Total Revenue Expenditures of All Districts from AFRs	$7,121,677,425	$7,447,555,299
Depreciated Asset Value Counted Sites	$20,575,117,177	$20,713,233,518
Assets to ADM	$22,102.93	$18,654.63
Long-Term Debt + LT Lease Commitments Counted Sties	$4,740,215,038	$5,128,615,502
Long-Term Lease Adjusted Debt to ADM	$5,092.20	$4,618.90
Shortfall in Dollars at Counted Sites	$15,834,902,139	$15,584,618,016
Surplus Property Value per ADM	$17,011	$14,036

NOTES

1. Civics education is woefully lacking in our public and charter schools. The efforts of the Dreyfuss Civic Initiative are recognized and supported here. See https://thedreyfussinitiative.org/.

2. Pogo was a Sunday morning paper cartoon character in the 1960s.

Chapter Twenty-Four

The Role of the Federal Government in Public Education

Supreme Court cases deciding the constitutionality of a state or communities' educational practices have been few and far between. When they occur, they reverberate through our public schools. Lower court decisions often impact how districts and charters can conduct business. Rules and regulations at a district often cite the state law to which the regulation correlates. States are often following federal rulings prior to writing their legislation.

The Supreme Court case that influenced what legally constitutes a "free and appropriate" public education in the last century dealt with the inherent problem of "separate but equal" educational opportunities (*Brown v. Board of Education*, 1954).

This Supreme Court ruling resulted in federal court–level decisions to federally enforce court-ordered bussing of students to schools that their parents did not choose. The idea was to open up schools in more affluent areas of a city (Boston) to students from the economically impoverished and racially segregated areas of the same city. The public did not respond well to court-ordered integration accomplished with court-ordered bussing.

In the early seventies, the exclusion of special-needs children from public education was debated following lawsuits brought by parents of special-needs students. The original cases were heard when New Jersey parents brought suit on behalf of their handicapped children. As a result of these parents' desire to see their children educated in the "lease restrictive environment" with their peers, Congress legislated that special-education students are entitled to a "Free and Appropriate" education.

The resulting law (Public Law 94-142)[1] expanded government's oversight of our special-needs populations. The impetus for this law was that grassroots effort by parents from New Jersey. This legislation was accompanied by claims by the law's detractors that the schools would "dumb down" their educational programs.

What really happened is that all children were now in the same classrooms as their special-education neighbors: a positive gain on the social capital side. Special-needs students continue to represent a costly increase on the economic side of the school funding equation. The law still mandates that the Local Education Agency (LEA: i.e., the district) is responsible for the education of children covered by this federal law.

If you are a Baby Boomer, you will recall the sometimes-cruel treatment of our special-needs children in the "good old days." As a firsthand observer, I witnessed our students taking care of and learning from their new classmates. PL 94-142 was good legislation designed to promote liberty and justice for all. However, PL 94-142 was never fully funded by the federal government. The local educational agency (LEA), as noted, is still the agency responsible for the placement and education of children who are covered under this law.

This placement can and does include placements in private educational programs. There is a solution for voucher organizers who claim the need for vouchers for special-needs children are not being met. The solution has been there since 1976. This topic will be expanded upon in the chapter on the goals of an American public education.

After World War I, it became apparent to the leaders of our democracy that illiteracy among the ranks of doughboys was a national defense issue. The National Defense Education Act of 1958 established funding based on our nation's need for literate soldiers and sailors, based on improved common schools, and to promote postsecondary education. The law was rightfully directly linked to a failed initiative in public schools at the time to teach "life skills."

When one reads early Friedman pieces on education, he roundly, and justifiably, criticizes this effort to move vocational training to the forefront at American high schools.[2] NDEA recognized the need for technically literate citizens.

> The purpose of the NDEA was to improve and strengthen all levels of the American school system and to encourage students to continue their education beyond high school. Specific provisions included scholarships and loans to students in higher education with loans to students preparing to be teachers and to those who showed promise in the curricular areas of mathematics, science, engineering, and modern foreign languages; grants to states for programs in mathematics, science, and modern foreign languages in public schools; the establishment of centers to expand and improve the teaching of languages; help to graduate students, including fellowships for doctoral students to prepare them to be professors at institutions of higher learning; assistance for the improve-

ment of guidance, counseling, and testing programs; provisions for research and experimentation in the use of television, radio, motion pictures, and related media for educational purposes; and the improvement of statistical services at the state level.

PRECEDENTS FOR FEDERAL INVOLVEMENT IN EDUCATION

"Supporters of the NDEA pointed to federal legislative precedents, such as the Morrill Act [3] in 1862, which granted land to the states that they could then sell to finance the establishment of colleges, and the Smith Hughes Act [4] in 1917, which funded vocational agricultural education programs. The NDEA differed from Smith-Hughes, however, in that professors of education, who had lost credibility by their espousal of, and involvement in, life adjustment education, played at best a minor role in the structure and operation of the NDEA."[5]

ORIGINS OF THE FEDERAL, STATE, AND LOCAL CONTROL DEBATES

Advocates of the NDEA contended that they were not interfering with the fundamental principle *that states and local communities*[6] were responsible for the conduct of American schooling and institutions of higher education.

Opponents maintained, however, that categorical aid, such as was proposed by the NDEA, would shape educational policy and would place the federal government in charge. This was not, in their view, a constructive policy on the part of the federal government.

In a 1964 amendment, the phrase "which have led to an insufficient proportion of our population educated in science, mathematics, and modern language and trained in technology" was deleted, as was the reference to giving preference in student loans to those preparing to teach and those with superior capacity in mathematics, science, engineering, or a modern foreign language.

The following year, the Catholic school where the author was a student in Emmaus, Pennsylvania, added "science" to its curriculum and in the following year "modern mathematics"[7] was introduced. Federal aid was now available for equipment and materials to be used in the instruction of an expanded list of subjects: "science, mathematics, history, civics, geography, modern foreign language, English or reading in public elementary or secondary schools."

All federal programs for education have always had the goal of *supplementing, not supplanting* the state and local funding sources for education.

The Catholic school the author attended was able to obtain equipment in order to supplement its educational programs as a part of the national goal of encouraging science, mathematics, and engineering, the precursor to STEM (Science, Technology, Engineering, and Mathematics) and STEAM (which added and recognized the value of the Arts into the STEM programs).

The goals of an American education have been shaped by these federal decisions. However, the main goal of an American public education has always been to educate and acculturate the future citizens of a democratic republic.

NOTES

1. The Education for All Handicapped Children Act (sometimes referred to using the acronyms EAHCA or EHA, or Public Law [PL] 94-142) was enacted by the United States Congress in 1975. The act was an amendment to Part B of the Education of the Handicapped Act enacted in 1966.
2. https://www.britannica.com/topic/National-Defense-Education-Act.
3. See also: Morrill Act.
4. www.britannica.com/topic/Smith-Hughes-Act.
5. https://www.britannica.com/topic/National-Defense-Education-Act.
6. https://www.merriam-webster.com/dictionary/communities.
7. Modern mathematics introduced elementary students to the logic of mathematics. This included an introduction to logic statements and the type of skills one needs to do computer coding. Bases 2, 8, and 16 were introduced to sixth and seventh graders. It is the author's opinion that this short-lived program introduced the computer geniuses of our generation to a way of thinking that then enabled them to capitalize on emerging technologies developed while we committed to putting a man on the moon before 1970.

Chapter Twenty-Five

The Goals of an American Public Education

John Dewey stated the goals of an American public education succinctly: "What the best and wisest parent wants for his own child, that must the community want for all of its children." This call to action did not mean that citizens should put their family and friends first while undermining the public good. That type of interpretation ignores the spirit of Dewey's work.

As an educator, the author can attest to the fact that the inclusion of all children in the classroom *benefits the entire spectrum of the bell curve*. Differentiated instruction is the key to challenging everyone in your classroom. As I reminded one of my teachers who complained about an identified ADHD (attention deficit with hyperactivity disorder) child not finishing his homework, "Mary, Danny is the one who will rush into your burning house in ten years and save you and then go back in for your dog."

Communities and our country need all our children's talents and gifts, not just those skills that come so readily to those in the 90th percentile on academic measures. Schooling together in common schools cements our relationship with our fellow community members.

In justifying the need for community (taxpayer) support for education based on what he termed the "neighborhood effect," even Milton Friedman understood the underlying importance of an educated populous to a republic: "A stabile and democratic society is impossible without a minimum degree of literacy and knowledge on the part of most citizens and without widespread acceptance of some common set of values"[1] Yes, he did say "a minimum degree of literacy and knowledge."

This is a far cry from the Libertarian Platform in 1980, which stated:

We condemn compulsory education laws, which spawn prison-like schools with many of the problems associated with prisons, and we call for the immediate repeal of such laws.

Until government involvement in education is ended, we support elimination within the governmental school system, of forced busing and corporal punishment. We further support immediate reduction of tax support for schools, and removal of the burden of school taxes from those not responsible for the education of children.[2]

COMMUNITIES MATTER

The word *community* in Dewey's educational statements is the second part of what should be the foundation of our republic's basic units: family and community.[3] It was a call for the community to provide each child with the type of education that the "best and brightest" parents in that community wanted for their children.

Dewey did not propose exempting citizens who were "not responsible for the education of children."[4] The second part of Dewey's quote is often left out: "*Any other ideal for our schools is narrow and unlovely, acted* upon, it destroys our democracy." The use of the words "*our schools*" is deliberate.

Privately held, under-water, overleveraged school choices are the unlovely result of the economic freedom of action granted to contracted educational businesses by deregulating the public's financial control of its public school resources. We have used an economic theory to set the wrong set of ideals for our public education efforts.

When the only social imperative for a business is to make money, the results, as can be seen in the data, are unlovely. We have created and enabled commerce without morality, and it is affecting our most precious commodity, our children. "What public good is served by a 'neighborhood effect' if the neighbors abandon their neighborhood schools and isolate their children from one another in privately owned and governed educational businesses?"

Fred Rogers understood the importance of neighborhoods and neighbors. He taught us to value Mr. McGregor's and other citizens' roles in the community. (If you are skeptical about that last claim, then how do you know Mr. McGregor was the postman in *Mr. Roger's Neighborhood*?)

Common public schools have been our communities' way of providing their neighborhood children with an American education before and since the country mandated compulsory education. Schooling alone,[5] in the title of this work, decries this loss of community voice in our children's education and the demise of our communities' local control of a democratic republic's free and appropriate education.

We are destroying and fragmenting our democracy under the guise of a "freedom to choose." This "freedom of choice" is based on the assumption that we are entitled to "our share" of the funds our state and community devotes to a public good.

Charter schools can and must be better than that. *At least 23 percent of those educational contractors are already demonstrating how this better version of charter schools can be achieved. They are in the 23 percent based on their academic and financial success and an ethical use of related party transactions to save money for their school through efficiency.*

These schools link themselves purposefully to the communities where they establish their businesses. Their business is education, not real estate acquisition.

CELEBRATE ALL OF OUR SUCCESSES

We need to stop beating up on one another if we are all in the business of educating Americans. This means that we acknowledge successes in all sectors of our educational endeavors. When the Beach Boys admonished us to "be true to our schools" in 1963, the graduation rate in the United States was at 76.5 percent. Using the newest way of measuring graduation rates, the statistics for 2017 state a graduation rate of 84 percent.[6] The rates dipped in the early part of the century but have been rising gradually since.

As a nation, we are educating more and more of our citizens in our common schools, both district and charter. We should all be proud of that accomplishment. Our public schools have taken on all students regardless of their starting point in life and turned them into full-fledged citizens of the republic. Job one for our public schools.

Our children did not disappoint us during and after 9/11. Public schools had something to do with their patriotism and valor. The schools that the Greatest Generation tried to provide for their descendants have produced another great generation. As one of their teachers, this author is proud of what our schools and his students have accomplished. Those schools need our support and care.

There is a saying: "If you think education is expensive, try ignorance." The road to universal publication has been long and tenuous.

The first state to have mandatory public education laws was Massachusetts, in 1852. The last state to establish compulsory education laws, Mississippi, did so in 1918. Massachusetts has been at this for a long time. They consistently place in the top three listings regarding academic performance at our public schools.

The high school graduation rate in the country in 1900 was 6.3 percent. By 1920, the rate was 16.8 percent.[7] By 1995, the year when the first states enacted legislation allowing charter contracting, the graduation rate was 84.5 percent.[8]

The benefits of a mandatory public education system are manifest in the rising graduation rates from 1900 onward. There should be no question about whether public education paid for by the public was a step toward "promoting the general welfare." It was.

We would be wise to consider that the same economists[9] who advocated for private ownership of our schools also disdained the idea of national parks held in trust for the public. The same economist, Milton Freidman, critiqued John F. Kennedy for his inaugural call to "Ask not what your country can do for you, but what you can do for your country" (Friedman, 1962).

We now have twenty-five-plus years of data on charter schools and vouchers. It is time we assess the effect of these "innovations" and decide whether they have been a disruptive innovation or a destructive invasion of our local public schools, a destructive force initiated by corporations, state governments, and the federal government.

It's time to reevaluate the charter and privatization model. We can and must come up with a better set of guidelines for our public charter schools and how we expend public funds for education.

We Baby Boomers have become like the Royal Astronomer in James Thurber's *The White Rabbit*. As we age, we are declaring that the stars are going out, when it is really our eyes that are failing. How did we become so disenchanted with something that served *us* so well?

Steven Brill, also a Baby Boomer, presents a poignant and powerful critique of how Baby Boomers have turned what used to be termed a meritocracy into a modern-day aristocracy (Brill 2018). Aristocracies and oligarchies are the antithesis of what a meritocracy is designed to combat. In a chapter discussing, "Why Nothing Works,"[10] Brill also points out the flaws in a public education system that appears incapable of firing and replacing inept teachers.

The author believes that when incompetent teachers are paid to report to what Brill calls "rubber rooms," it is a failure of the supervision and evaluation process. *That is, it is a failure of management, not teachers' unions.*

Appointing inexperienced (i.e., those with no educational background) CEOs to oversee this supervision and evaluation process is a step in the wrong direction. Experience in charters where nepotism occurs at the teacher and management levels points to evidence that suggests this form of management is even more ineffective at eliminating poor performances.

Charter firms, in the author's experience, took on additional members of the charter holder's family and friends when there was a change at the charter holder level. This placed middle management in the untenable position of supervising "the boss's children."

Experience also showed that it was difficult, if not impossible, to terminate incompetent staff members who happened to be members of the owner's family or congregation. A particularly egregious example of this conflict of interest was when the owner hired an uncertified "new teacher" from their congregation at $50K, when that charter started certified teachers at $32K. The logic given was that *he had to support his family*. The rest of the staff were females, some single mothers.

We Baby Boomers have led the charge to promote "school choice" and government subsidies for privately owned "public" schools—an entitlement mentality applied to a public good. We have replaced unionized public schools with community-held properties ruled by crony capitalism and oligarchies.

The road we are following is taking us on a path where schooling alone in separate "public" school choices is the norm rather than being true to our schools. It is a road to financial, political, and social perdition.

As Kurt Vonnegut would say, "Enough already."

> *"Don't it always seem to go, that you don't know what you've got till it's gone."*
>
> —Joni Mitchell

NOTES

1. Friedman, 1962, p. 86.
2. http://lpedia.org/1980_National_Platform#4._Education.
3. We include religious, civic, and recreational organizations in our definition of community.
4. This statement put full responsibility for educating our children on the parents. The economic theory was that this would discourage parents from having children they could not afford.
5. Putnam, 2000. Putnam's book *Bowling Alone: The Collapse and Revival of American Community*.
6. https://www.edweek.org/ew/articles/2017/12/07/whats-behind-the-record-rises-in-us.html.

7. http://www.safeandcivilschools.com/research/graduation_rates.php.
8. https://nces.ed.gov/pubs/dp95/97473-3.asp.
9. The Greatest Generation included Dr. Friedman. Dr. Friedman famously supported a volunteer military, arguing with General Westmoreland during the Vietnam era regarding Westmoreland's statement that a purely volunteer force would be the equivalent of a mercenary army. Friedman responded by asking whether an army of slaves would be better. He was also known for his work developing and applying statistical analysis to war research (1942 through 1945).
10. *Tailspin: The People and Forces behind America's Fifty-Year Fall—and Those Fighting to Reverse It* (Brill, 2018). See pp. 165–168.

Chapter Twenty-Six

Cashing In—Greed Is "Good"

> One of the great mistakes is to judge policies and programs by their intentions rather than their results.
>
> —Milton Friedman

On July 15, 2018, the *Arizona Republic* published one of its continuing series of award-winning investigations regarding charter school finances in Arizona. The title of the piece was *"Cashing In on Charter Schools."* The article was typical of what comes up when a search of "charter school finances" is entered as a search engine query.

Arizona receives an "A" rating for its charter laws from the leading charter school advocacy group, the Center for Educational Reform. The executive director of CER, Jeanne Allen, is quoted as saying, "Arizona gets high marks from charter-school advocates because it provides operators with autonomy and encourages them to innovate."[1]

This part of this treatise is not presented to disparage the reporting, or the answers given by the charter holder, in the article being quoted here. It is presented as evidence of the current *mindsets* in the industry and the fourth estates' perception about the current way charter schools are conducting business.

The federal government has some of the same financial accountability concerns discussed in this chapter.

The U.S. Department of Education (USDOE), *a staunch supporter of charter expansion*, is also concerned about financial responsibility in the charter sector. Despite the stated antigovernment schools' rhetoric, the charter industry receives billions of dollars in federal funding. The financial accounting for that funding is not meeting GAO standards. In a 2016 General Accounting Office (GAO) report to the USDOE, the GAO noted the inability of the USDOE to track how federal funding was being spent.

A particular concern in that report centered on charter corporations' use of Educational Management Organizations (EMOs) aka CMOs (Charter Management Organizations). The report found:

> That the Department (USDOE) did not have effective internal controls to evaluate and mitigate the risk that charter school relationships with CMOs pose to Department program objectives. The Department did not have controls to identify and address the risks related to CMO relationships because it did not believe the risk to be materially different than risks presented by other grantees that received Department funds. In addition, Department officials stated that the Office of Innovation and Improvement (OII) uses a risk-based strategy in the monitoring and administration of CSP (Charter School Program) grants. (Source: https://www2.ed.gov/about/offices/list/oig/auditreports/fy2016/a02m0012.pdf)

A General Accounting Office official summed up the effects of lobbying and government contracting: *"It's not really a matter of personal corruption; it is just an insidious culture that is corrupting."*

The intent of this author is not to accuse the people who run charters as businesses of personal corruption. It is, however, a statement about an insidious corporate culture *that is corrupting charter finances.*

When the public reads stories regarding what is going on with charter financials, they are shocked. They are re-shocked when they hear that those financial activities are all legal. It will be telling to see what the current secretary of education does with the contents of this GAO report. We predict that it will be buried.

THE PROFIT MOTIVE: A CASE IN POINT

During an interview with Glenn Way, the owner of several charters known as the American Leadership Academies, was questioned about his companies' business practices by Craig Harris. Mr. Harris is an investigative reporter from the *Arizona Republic* (and *USA Today*). He asked the following: "Do you think it's appropriate to develop charter schools and make money?"

Mr. Way responded, "Absolutely. It's no different than building a Walmart, CVS, or Walgreens."

Mr. Way's answer is brutally frank, *and his assertion is correct.* Charter school construction and the profits to be made in that arena *are no different from building a Walmart, CVS, or Walgreens.* Charter law authorizes this type of related party bid-free transaction, and it allows the owner to profit from this transaction during the construction phase and all other phases of development.

In twenty-one states, charter law also entitles the owner to all financial benefits that come from owning the real estate assets of a charter school. Owning the real estate and leasing it back to the primary business is a business fact of life. A business fact that Ray Kroc, the founder of McDonald's, learned quickly as he developed the franchise and took over the McDonald's name from his "partners," Dick and Maurice McDonald.

However, we note that those non-charter free-market businesses that were cited by Mr. Way (*Walmart, CVS, or Walgreens*) and today's McDonald's franchisees do not have access to tax-free bonds. They use commercial borrowing or finance their real estate purchase with their own capital. Some, like Mr. Way, have figured out how to capitalize even further from the construction and leasing of charter schools.

Mr. Way does not use tax-free bonding for his schools. He has an interest in a construction firm that buys and builds charter schools, sells the school to another firm (a related party), and then leases the properties to the charter group held by Mr. Way and his associates. That firm "manages the schools and provides leased teachers to those schools."

Chuck Essigs, a public school business executive (Arizona Association of School Business Managers), is also quoted in the article: "There are time-tested reasons why traditional public school officials must adhere to Arizona's 112-page state procurement manual, which requires bidding for construction projects and other contracts: They protect taxpayers from being overcharged. It is public money, and you have a fiduciary responsibility to make sure you are getting value," he said.[2]

Those statements as they relate to regulated school districts are correct.

Mr. Essigs also stated, "Charter schools were not started to earn profits."

Mr. Essigs is misinformed.

Making a profit is exactly what charter schools are now designed to do, as they operate as free-market contracted educational businesses. The charter laws make them independent contractors "freed" from the regulations that guide public schools on the acceptable use of taxpayer dollars. Charter schools are contracted businesses providing an educational service.

The theory behind "choice" is an economic theory of action applied to an educational marketplace. The justification for using tax dollars to private providers of educational "services" was a major thesis put forward by Milton Friedman in *Capitalism and Freedom*. At the time, in the 1970s, Friedman was also critiquing the business world for putting an emphasis on a business' social responsibility.

> There is one and only one social responsibility of business—to use its resources and engage in activities designed to increase its profits so long as it stays within the rules of the game, which is to say, engages in open and free competition without deception or fraud.[3]
>
> –Milton Friedman

When state legislatures make rules of the game that remove the legal definitions of deception of fraud that are in those regulations, then *there is no illegal deception or fraud*. The practice has gone legitimate based on the new legislation deregulating the rules. In reality, deregulation of the financial constraints on educational spending removed the financial "rules of the game" Dr. Friedman speaks about from one segment of the competition for public educational funding while leaving the same rules in place at the "competition" districts.

Charter contractors and private schools don't have to follow the financial rules enforced at districts. They have been "deregulated."

This statement is not being made to complain about the regulations and procurement processes to which public schools must adhere. Those rules are there for a reason. Those rules are there to regulate behavior, not legislate morality. As a nation, our political conversations have moved from being civil and at the same time combative to a focus on the combat rather than the context of the subject we are debating. Public spending on education and our commitment to educate all American children is too important for this type of political discourse.

We are supposed to be gaining an innovation bonus from this self-inflicted financial chaos in an economic model gone awry. There are things that gain from disorder as Nasisim Nicholas Teleb points out in "Anti-fragile" (Taleb, 2014). It is the contention of this author that the gains from this last change from an educational philosophy driving our educational investments to an economic theory based on a free-market economics model has created the unplanned economic chaos in the data.

That deliberately created chaos has not led to any *substantial gain* in educational outcomes and at the same time has weakened the financial health of our systems for funding education. Financial entropy is occurring as a result of this lack of fiscal oversight. A fiscal death spiral fueled by overleveraged debt is threatening charters and public districts primary sources of revenue.

Taleb also states that "When you see fraud and do not say fraud, then you are a fraud."

The public *is being defrauded in this economic model*. The definition of *fraud* is to illegally obtain money from someone by *deception*. Making things that would be illegal in one segment (districts) of a "free market" illegal, while at the same time legitimizing the same practice at the competition educational contractors' firms, makes no sense.

Does this sound like an "open and free" market?

The financial rules of the game are rigged. When legislators participate in this legalized heist by becoming educational contractors, one wonders aloud, Who made up these new rules of the game? The economic theory driving this model was further articulated in 1976 with the publication of *The Theory of the Firm*.

THE THEORY OF THE FIRM

Friedman's students and disciples, Michael Jensen and William Meckling, developed a "theory of the firm"[4] in 1976. That theory formulaically described the manager's responsibility as an agent of the firm to *ensure corporate profitability*. This seminal work is the source of some of the logic behind compensation packages that reward CEOs with corporate stock and options in the private sector. Charters and private schools are in this sector.

The case for this interpretation is magnified when the charter is a for-profit charter school. CEOs compensation packages are tied to the financial performance of the firm. The distributions noted in this report are being paid to them *because they are also the stockholders and in most cases the charter holder (owner)*.

Here's how the theory of the firm works in practice when applied to a public good. The sole stock holder[5] of the "for-profit" Benjamin Franklin Schools converted the charter school subsidiaries of his business group from "for-profit" to nonprofit status. The sole owner, who had bought out his partners over several years, then cashed in on his owner's equity built up during the twenty years that he personally guaranteed the school's debts. The owner's equity was also used during the partner buyouts. Mr. Farnsworth, the CEO of the firm, declared, "I make no apologies for being successful" (attributed to Arizona state legislator Eddie Farnsworth in the *Arizona Republic*).

The quote is a symptom of the issue. Mr. Farnsworth is the messenger. He is a legislator, currently a state senator; however, he did not participate in writing the charter laws. To his credit, he has voted "no" several times on legislation that would have benefited him financially. Mr. Farnsworth is an honest player in this marketplace *as it is defined in legislation*. The problem isn't Mr. Farnsworth's honesty or business acumen. The problem is an economic model applied to what we know as public education.

The economic theory of action articulated in the theory of the firm is *fundamentally* based on the belief that "greed is good."[6] Charter laws allow the

CEO to be owner of the firm and to either serve on the corporate board or, as in some for-profit firms, all three, that is, as charter holder, corporate board member, and member of the governing board.

Responding to a report by the *Arizona Republic* critical of the owners of another large charter group, BASIS, having the money to buy an expensive condo in New York City, the leader of the Arizona Charter Association called Mr. Harris's question "un-American."

That critique by the head of the charter association is correct.

It would be un-American *if she were describing an America where capitalism is not only an economic theory of action, but the definition of what education in an American democracy is all about.*

The purpose of a business according to the operational economic theory *is* to make money. For whom? The shareholders of the corporation.

In charters, this is most often the CEO/owner. The problem isn't the owner's spending their legally obtained profits, *it's the economic model that sets this ability to profit from education into motion. Charter and voucher legislation at the state and federal levels have allowed a capitalist economic theory to trump our educational goals of educating American citizens in a democratic republic.*

We, the public, have allowed state legislatures and the federal government to use legislative power to usurp and replace what used to be a locally controlled, community-based, public school system.

This hostile corporate[7] takeover of public education is based on and guided by an economic theory of action that equates our capitalist economic system with our political system, which is a democratic republic. A conundrum.

Education has been converted into a contracted service rather than a community's public service to its children. The state and federal governments have done this through state and federal legislation and an intentionally deregulated set of financial "rules."

The effort to privatize public education has been financed and promoted by ALEC, corporate interests, chambers of commerce, and lobbyists for "charter advocacy groups" determined to privatize our public schools and other government services. This theory of economic action has been packaged and sold as an educational and financial "innovation." One of those innovations is touted as the ability to run schools like businesses (Ash, 2013; Green, 2017).

Is that the goal of an American public school education? The director of Oxfam International, Winnie Byanylma, recently said: "We should rid ourselves of the belief that business innovation inherently means social progress."

Public education is not, nor was it designed to be, a capitalistic business. It is a public service (good) provided to educate our children. Those practitioners in the charter marketplace who are in the 23 percent who are identified as practicing in a socially responsible way, easily voiced their moral compasses when the author interviewed them on their school's posted mission statements.

The model we are using believes that educational progress occurs as a result of business innovation and competition. It is never stated as the primary goal but it is implied in the theories regarding free markets and rising wealth in the private sector. "A rising tide raises all ships." The trouble with that is that some of us don't have a raft, boat, or a ship.

Teaching is a vocation, not a contracted service paid to an employment subsidiary of the charter. As Christa McAuliffe so eloquently said, "I touch the future; I teach." This is a far cry from "we are running schools like a business." Christa, a fellow New Hampshire teacher, spoke to what really motivates the people who enter the teaching profession.

That motivation isn't profit driven. Rather, it is as Parker Palmer has noted: because they have "the heart of a teacher" (Palmer, 2017; Palmer, 2007).

We are not talking about trivial profit margins and those charter operators that are barely eking by while providing their communities with a choice. We are talking about profiteering from a public good. The public does not support profiteering, whether it is in military contracts or in our public schools. We still have a chance to do something about this latest privatization of a public good. This requires using some of our political capital.

The free press, to its credit, continues to call out this "legal" corporate behavior in a deregulated free market. On September 11, 2018, the *Arizona Republic* reported on Mr. Farnsworth's real estate transactions as just that, real estate transactions.

> East Valley charter school owner and state lawmaker Eddie Farnsworth is poised for a payday of up to $30 million after the Arizona State Board for Charter Schools approved the transfer of his for-profit charter school chain to a newly formed non-profit company on Monday.
>
> In a 10-0 vote,[8] the board OK'd Farnsworth's request to transfer the charter from the for-profit Benjamin Franklin Charter School, which operates four campuses, to a Queen Creek, Arizona non-profit company with the same name.
>
> That move will allow Farnsworth, a lifetime Republican state representative,[9] to sell the campuses-paid for with state tax dollars-to the non-profit company for between $11.8 million and $29.9 million, according to Charter Board records (audits).
>
> The figures vary because of conflicting financial audits Benjamin Franklin provided to the Charter Board. Farnsworth declined to clarify the discrepancy.

Author's comment: The Arizona State Board for Charter Schools *had no legal choice* except to vote like they did. *They didn't have the legal authority to do anything else.* Mr. Farnsworth did not break any Arizona laws.

The state-level authorizers of our charter schools need to be given the tools to do their jobs. This means tightening up the financial rules of the game.

The public's only recourse when they read of these transactions is to "vote with their feet." Parents do still have that choice.

There has been no mass exodus from the Benjamin Franklin Schools since the *Arizona Republic* story. Parents made their choice. If they agreed with the conclusions of the *Arizona Republic* article, they had a right to exercise their right to choose by leaving. Stated another way, if parents disagreed with the financial practices being used at their charter contractor's schools, they could exit that school. They didn't.

This does not mean that they didn't express—that is, voice—their dismay to the owners of those schools. The power of a citizen's voice in a democratic republic was underestimated and misjudged by Dr. Friedman's thesis (Hirschman, 1970; Palmer, 2000).

Exiting is only one form of how citizens in a republic express their opinions. Voice and loyalty are equally important in how we make consumer decisions when we have the freedom to choose. The customers at Mr. Farnsworth's schools have by and large remained loyal to his schools.

NEW RULES

The "new rules" for charter schools and private schools accepting vouchers or tax credit scholarships allow private ownership of our public school facilities by corporations who are then free to profiteer from a public good. The new rules allow, and de facto encourage with tax incentives, the unfettered use of related party transactions with subsidiary firms. The public is told that this creates "efficiency and money savings."

What it really creates is what is seen in these news articles and in the raw financial data.

Those types of transactions are not what the public wants or expects for its public schools. Commerce without conscience still violates norms most citizens hold in their personal theories about justice and fair play. The playing field varies from state to state.

As of October 2018, there are forty-three states and the District of Columbia that allow charter schools in their jurisdiction. *Twenty-one of those states allow "for-profit" charter schools and/or "for-profit" educational management companies. Thirty-three of those forty-four provide tax-free bonding opportunities for charter school property acquisition.*[10] *The majority.*

"In a brief interview with the *Arizona Republic*, Mr. Farnsworth said he is deserving of a big financial reward because he took the risk in 1995 to start his charter school chain and personally guaranteed millions of dollars in loans to launch Benjamin Franklin." He offered, "No apologies for being successful."

Author's note: Mr. Farnsworth was the source of the quote, "We designed it to work that way," referenced earlier. The author questioned him during a Meet the Candidates night in 2016. *To his credit, Mr. Farnsworth does run his schools like a business and he provides his teachers with Arizona Retirement System benefits and bonuses when they exceed expectations (just like a real business). He also put up his own money*[11] *to get the charters he runs started.* Good for him.

His four schools get "As and Bs" on the academic rating scales. Those schools are located in an "A"-rated district. He is delivering on his contract to provide educational services.

After stories published by the *Republic* and reports on charter financials by the Grand Canyon Institute and others, the public asks, "How is this all possible?"

Answer: A public good is being driven by an economic theory of action in this segment of the "free market" and the general public's belief that that economic theory works.

Repeating what educators have been saying for years, *"Schools are not businesses."*

Police departments, fire departments, and our armed forces aren't businesses, either. These are all fields that are not staffed by people who are seeking to make a fortune. We know this intuitively.

Kurt Vonnegut, while addressing graduates of Fredonia College in 1978, succinctly stated a fact about the type of person who goes into teaching: "Most of you are preparing to enter fields unattractive to greedy persons, such as education and the healing arts. Teaching, may I say, is the noblest profession of all in a democracy" (Vonnegut, 2016).

Becoming a worker in a service industry is not a business decision. The trouble is, we have made the field attractive to greedy persons by letting an economic theory of action take precedence over our political and social contracts with our children's education and our communities.

What have been the results of this economic theory of action?

Trusting our schools to an economic theory has led to a major transfer of formerly publicly held real estate and control of our children's education to the private sector. It is time to evaluate the results rather than the espoused theories of "choice." Who is choosing (private corporations), and who is losing (the community)?

Experience in the industry, district schools, and private businesses allowed the author to see how the economic theory really works in action.

It is clear "who it works for": the taxpaying public.

I see who it works for.

—Gracie Allen**

**Gracie Allen was responding to George Burns's explanation of how 50 percent of what she had went to him, and 50 percent of what he had went to her. The comedy bit started with George asking Gracie to take out a dollar. This was followed by a routine where he asked her for half of the dollar she had, and then handed half of what he had back to her. Gracie looks at her quarter and George asks, "Do you see how it works?"

Gracie's replies, "I see who it works for." —From a recording of Burns and Allen

NOTES

1. IRS form 990 https://www.guidestar.org/FinDocuments/2016/521/847/2016-521847187-0ec3911d-9.pdf documentation showed that the executive director of the Center for Educational Reform earned $217,497 a year in FY 2016. This was up from $98,000 in FY 2015, when she served as president. The executive director that year received compensation of $148,000. A group that would have great issue with public school districts giving extraordinary pay raises to public school administrators more than doubled Ms. Allen's compensation in one year. Ms. Allen is also listed as the founder of this nonprofit company: founder, president, and then executive director.

2. https://www.azcentral.com/story/news/local/arizona-education/2018/07/11/american-leadership-academy-charter-school-founder-glenn-way-nets-millions/664210002/.

3. https://www.colorado.edu/studentgroups/libertarians/issues/friedman-soc-resp-business.html.

4. Jensen, 1976.) *Theory of the Firm, Managerial Behavior, Agency Costs, and Ownership Structure.*

5. Mr. Farnsworth, using owner's equity in the company, had bought out his partners during the prior fiscal years. Source: Audit data from FY 2014 through FY 2017.

6. The expression was made famous in the movie *Wall Street*, which drew on Friedman's Economic Theories. Ironically, charter schools that consider themselves bastions of moral legitimacy ignore one of the seven deadly sins recognized by most "Christian" religions, avarice, aka greed.

7. Hostile because the intent is to replace public schools entirely. This is evident in states with charters where developers are allowing charter schools to set up their schools in new developments without consulting with the school districts they are located in. That is, there is no choice because a monopoly of charter schools has been established. As one might suspect, there is often collusion with the builder regarding

who gets the contract to build the new charter along with payments to the company that "facilitated" the transaction. Source: Experience.

8. The board was legally obligated under current financial rules to allow this sale. To their credit, the ASBCS is working to tighten up their financial control of the charter marketplace in Arizona.

9. Mr. Farnsworth was not in the legislature when the original charter laws were passed. He does, however, vote on bills that potentially impact his companies' bottom line. There are cases where Mr. Farnworth voted against items that would have positively impacted his personal finances.

10. Source: collated data on charter school laws in the United States from multiple sources.

11. These loans are set to be replaced with IDA tax-free bonds on the property for a far greater value than the properties are currently worth. A large tax break to the bondholders ensures that less money will be available to the state to support these charter contracts. In addition, Mr. Farnsworth's properties will be no longer paying property taxes. Smart business moves that detract from the public good.

Chapter Twenty-Seven

An Educational Vision versus an Economic Theory of Action

For over twenty-five years, we have allowed our public schools to be guided by an economic theory of action rather than an *educational vision* regarding what an American education should provide to its future citizens. This work questions the general economic principles laid out in state and federal efforts to privatize public education.

We have asked two questions of the data:

- *What have the promoters of charter schools done with the freedom over their budgets, staffing, curricula, and other operations?*
- *What is the result of eliminating the substantial conformity of governance and finance rules for operating schools (financed from taxpayers' dollars) on the governance and finances of these entities?*

The answers presented in the data are that this contracted model of education is "narrow and unlovely." Acted upon, it can and is destroying our democracy. That destruction is occurring economically, politically, and in the destruction of the social capital of our communities.

The current debate about public education in our democratic republic often misses these critical issues and factors.

Are American students attending public (district and charter) schools becoming well-educated citizens of our democratic republic or well-schooled widgets where those children's education is the "product" the contractors are "delivering" in a capitalistic economic system?

When the author was in the "charter business," he often asked this question when a particularly troubling financial decision was made by management:

"Is this a business decision or an educational decision?"

Each time the response was, "It's a business decision." Economics drove the company's agenda. A corporate makeover of public education causes this type of business-first mindset.

Michael Fabricant and Michelle Fine refer to the process of privatizing public schools as "the corporate makeover of public education." In the first chapter of their book by the same title, the authors start with a discussion of the organizational reframing of education under an economic theory of action: "What we consider 'public' in public education in the United States is under construction. . . . Our commitment to shared fates, democratic participation, and concerns for equity . . . are in jeopardy" (Fabricant and Fine 2013).

This view was also present in *The Changing Politics of Education: Privatization and the Disposed Lives Left Behind* (Fabricant and Fine 2013). These innovators (and this author counts himself as one) are under a moral obligation to stand up and speak out regarding this hostile corporate takeover of our public schools. There are multiple voices sounding the alarm. The real innovators are speaking up.

In the preface to Fine's *Charter Schools and the Corporate Makeover of Public Schools,* Deborah Meier, an innovator who brought change to New York City public schools, wrote:

> In light of the privatizing zeal to "save" public schools, I have had opportunity for reflections upon whether some of my earlier work may have inadvertently carved a path toward what we now witness. Like Michelle Fine, I was deeply involved in the small schools movement which may now be seen as the forerunner of today's charter schools.

What was not envisioned by earlier innovators from the teaching profession was niche schools designed by corporations for a particular demographic or social class housed in privately owned, publicly funded "public schools."

After working in charter schools in both New Hampshire and then for ten years in Arizona, I initiated an in-depth academic study designed to answer two questions. Questions designed to test the realities of the "economic theories of action" behind privately owned public schools were developed and researched.

We also asked the following of the data: "How did the espoused theories regarding privatizing public education play out over the past twenty-five years in these private entities' theories in action?" We looked at the results, not the intentions of the efforts to privatize and contract out public education.

The disappointments with how charter schools have evolved in this country are reflected in practitioners' comments in the introduction and within this work, but they *have not led those charter innovators to give up on the idea of public charter schools.*

Reflective practitioners also acknowledge that there are issues in public schools that need correcting. However, the real innovators in the charter movement are also tired of the realities of an economic theory of action driving the "charter marketplace." This disappointment is voiced almost daily in articles published across the country.

Dwight Eisenhower warned the country about the military-industrial complex during his farewell address. We are now in year twenty-five of an era of corporate education slowly taking over our public schools.

We hire military contractors to perform things we used to expect were taken care of by our tax-financed military. The historic name for such subcontracted soldiers is *"mercenaries."*

We now allow subcontracted corporate controlled-teachers to "educate" the future leaders of our republic at privately-owned "public school choices." We can do better than that.

Chapter Twenty-Eight
Philosophical Dissonance

The details in the 1980 Libertarian Party Educational Platform lay bare the fact that we have been deceived by charter advocacy organizations about the real plan to destroy all forms of publicly sponsored (i.e., publicly funded), locally controlled education.

When did we get so cynical about public education?

The real national effort to allow parents the "freedom to choose" started in the late sixties and early seventies. It occurred during a period when public reaction to *Brown v. Board of Education* in 1954 and the bussing of students in Boston were flashpoints for those who disagreed with these court-ordered desegregation efforts in our nation's public schools.

We have always been evolving our ideas regarding what constitutes an equal educational opportunity in this republic.

THE FIGHT FOR EQUALIZED OPPORTUNITY FUNDING

Most states had their funding of education tested during state supreme court cases challenging the distribution of funding from the state. The grounds for most of these successful cases were the unequal amount of funding available at the local level.[1] The lawsuits sought to equalize opportunity to ensure that each child had a fair and equitable amount of money funding their free and appropriate public school education.

In Arizona, the ruling led to the Equalized Funding Formula used by the state to equalize its distribution of educational spending based on a community's ability to fund education without overburdening property holders. The discrepancies cited by advocates for equalization included towns with a low property tax base. These communities were taxing the properties in their towns at a higher rate than communities with a larger property tax base.

As a country, we have always believed in equal opportunity under the law—or have we?

The first edition of *Capitalism and Freedom* by Dr. Milton Friedman included this byline:

> A Leading Economist's View of the Proper Role of Competitive Capitalism (Friedman, 1962).

The ideal of competitive capitalism as a solution set for what ails public education is part of Friedman's and Hayek's propositions regarding the relationship between a "free" person (*man* was the term used in the original) and his government (Hayek, 1944).

Which leaders from the 1960s are we choosing to follow?

During the 1960s, Dr. Friedman was highly critical of John F. Kennedy's call to: "Ask not what your country can do for you; ask what you can do for your country."

Dr. Friedman vehemently disagreed with JFK's call to service to country and community.

Friedman wrote the following in the introduction to his free-market economics treatise on competitive capitalism: "In a much-quoted passage in his inaugural address, President Kennedy said, 'Ask not what your country can do for you—ask what you can do for your country.' It is a striking sign of the temper of our times that the controversy about this passage centered on its origin and not on its content."**

> Neither half of the statement expresses a relation between the citizen and his government that is worthy of the ideals of free men in a free society. The paternalistic, "what you can do for your country" implies that government is the patron, the citizen the ward, a view that is at odds with the free man's belief in his own responsibility for his own destiny. The organismic "what you can do for your country" implies that government is the master or the deity, the citizen, the servant or the votary.[2]

Translation: *Ask not what you can do for your country, but what your country can do for you.*

The effect of this juxtaposition of the original results in an entitlement mindset of "me first."

**Author's note: Several commentators at the time questioned the original source of the phrase used by President Kennedy. Ironically, his headmaster, George St. John, at the private Choate School in Connecticut, is generally believed to be the source of these words.[3] Irony abounds as one finds out that a defender of privatizing public education takes to task the words of a private school teacher uttered by a president advocating for citizens to put country first.

Dr. Friedman's original economic hypothesis[4] supporting free-market approaches to education in a capitalist country are articulated in his 1955 paper, "*The Role of Government in Education.*" That paper called for vouchers that could be used in either public or private schools. In that work, Friedman justified using government-raised funds, that is, tax revenues, for this purpose.

Friedman's works, along that of with the well-known economist, Hayek's *The Road to Serfdom*, implied that there are economic theories that can and should determine how a free society provides an education to their citizens (Hayek 1980, 1982). Hayek also taught at the University of Chicago when Milton Friedman was there, along with likeminded economists Frank H. Knight, Henry C. Simons, Lloyd W. Mints, Aaron Director, and George J. Stigler.

In what was termed as the "neighborhood effect," Friedman argued that an individual's education benefits not only himself, but also society generally, when it makes him a better citizen (author's emphasis). This argument was used to justify using taxpayer resources to pay for an individual's publicly supported education.[5]

The "neighborhood effect" aspect of Friedman's thesis is seldom included in arguments used by the charter industry as a part of their manifestos.

It has been replaced with "Freedom to Choose," with educational contractors providing the choices paid with tax resources collected for the public welfare.

Hayek's *Road to Serfdom* has morphed into roads lined with educational contractor's privately held schools where the serfs pay the taxes and fees, but don't own the properties where we educate our children. We need to ask, "Who are the serfs, and who is the land holder?"

The free-market business model espoused by the American Legislative Exchange Council and the Center for Educational Reform is their posited economic, social, and political solution to all of our educational ills. The model's hallmark, capitalistic economic competition for consumer-based choices, is presented as a financially self-correcting method of providing educational opportunity to our citizens. It is presented as a way to "empower parents."

> Instead of throwing more money at the problem, it's time to let parents take back control over their children's educations by allowing them to apply competitive pressure to schools and educational providers. Innovative, parent-empowering choices such as charter schools, voucher programs, tax credit scholarships,

homeschool, and education savings accounts allow each child the opportunity to reach his or her potential. (Source: ALEC Webpage)

Friedman's and ALEC's economic theory of action launched state legislative actions in the late 1980s to authorize charter schools and vouchers in individual states. The timeline is important. The 1980 educational platform of the Libertarian Party and the party's vice-presidential candidate, David Koch, called for the dismantling of all public education. Right to work laws were next, followed by declarations of open enrollment[6] at existing districts. Shortly thereafter, in 1991, the first charter laws took effect in Minnesota.

In a 2012 (April 24) *Washington Post* article, Rachel Weiner identified the origin and composition of the original ALEC organization: "ALEC was formed in 1973 by conservative activists Lou Barnett and Paul Weyrich (who also founded the Heritage Foundation), along with then-State Rep. Henry Hyde (R-Ill.) and other Republican legislators. The goal: bring conservative *economic policy ideas to the state and local level.*"

A special report by "PR Watch" on ALEC's Funding and Spending provides the details of this organization, noting that, "Since CMD, (the Center for Media and Democracy), first exposed ALEC in 2011, more than 100 corporations have dropped ALEC, including Ford, Coca-Cola, Wal-Mart, General Electric, and Google." As a result of that ongoing investigation and other reporting, CMD is often contacted by whistleblowers wanting to make a difference.

CMD has also researched the array of groups that are part of ALEC, including numerous Koch-funded entities and national and state "think tanks" that are affiliated with the State Policy Network. The Center for Media and Democracy is listed as a progressive organization.

The phrase *"government schools"* has been derisively applied to our locally controlled, democratically elected, school board–governed schools. Using ideological rhetoric that compares this form of "local government"-run organization to the communist state-run schools of the 1950s is a travesty. The country's locally governed public schools fit Jefferson's oft-stated support of education for enlightening members of a democratic republic. Jefferson knew and stated often that universal education was the true corrective of abuses of constitutional power.

> I know no safe depository of the ultimate powers of the society but the people themselves; and if we think them not enlightened enough to exercise their control with a wholesome discretion, the remedy is not to take it from them, but to inform their discretion by education. This is the true corrective of abuses of constitutional power.
>
> —Thomas Jefferson to W. Jarvis, 1820

State charter laws that take local boards out of the decision making regarding what type of educational opportunities their communities will support and cherish take this "choice" away from the local community.

Charters that keep the community in their planning and as a vital part of their mission tend to also have local governing boards. This was the case in only 23 percent of the charter governance structures analyzed.

Enough already!

NOTES

1. Most local funds for education come from a local property tax. The tax base is the total value of the taxable property in a district. The argument was that states should be supplementing this source based on the district's ability to pay for education. The results of these efforts constitute the Equalized Valuation Rates used in most states as a measure of how much each area receives in state funding.

2. Milton Friedman, in the Introduction to *Capitalism and Freedom*.

3. http://www.dailymail.co.uk/news/article-2056020/JFK-stole-ask-country-speech-old-headmaster.html.

4. The word *hypothesis* is used here because Friedman was proposing a known economic theory, free-market capitalism, to a field that was a government-funded public good. Economic theory in this book is used because free-market capitalism is an economic theory.

5. The most recent remarks at the Mises Institute, a Libertarian think tank, take issue with Friedman's justification of using tax revenues to pay for an individual's education. This is consistent with the Libertarian 1980 platform on education.

6. An unfunded mandate in Arizona, because unlike charters, Equalized Valuation and extra revenues do not follow a child to a district accepting the child for open enrollment. The cost is borne by the local taxpayer in property-rich towns that accept open enrollment students as they receive little funding directly from the states in an equalized-funding formula.

Chapter Twenty-Nine

Enough Already

The financial theories that were used to justify government contractual service spending on charter schools (the "neighborhood effect") and the theories in use in the marketplace do not match up.

When espoused theories do not match the theories in use in a free market, conservatives, moderates, and liberals should begin to question the model.

Is it what we are espousing—free-market economic theory—or how we are implementing the operating theory in this market, public education, that is causing this dissonance?

By any practical measure of financial analysis, the economic model is an economic failure.

It is also poor educational policy for a democratic republic.

Politically, the model has disrupted a political process that has served us well in the past: political leadership at the local level followed by state office followed by national office. When we bypassed one of the most important local-level election issues, school boards, we weakened the link between civic engagement at the local level and the state and federal levels. All politics are not local anymore, because we have bypassed one of the main functions of local government, providing local educational opportunities.

A dangerous precedent is being set as states usurp local control of public education. This overreach has resulted in state regulations that undermine local communities' abilities to manage and determine what their schools look like. We, the public, need to ask, "What's next, state control of locally contracted police and fire departments?"

Recent legislation limiting petitioned ballot articles to the state while placing onerous rules on what constitutes a "legal signature" on those petitions are signs that our First Amendment rights to petition *our* government are also under attack. In an age when we have accepted security searches and requirements to present our papers to federal agents when we travel, we have accepted loss of local control of our public schools without a fight.

When we, the people, elect to choose our way out of our community schools, we are abandoning one of the core institutions in our civic life, a common educational system that brings all sectors of our community together.

This separation from publicly provided education *is and always was a parent's right*. What is not a right is to take the money the taxpayers have provided for a *public education* with you.

There are already mechanisms in place to ensure your child is placed in the least restrictive environment, including private placements, in the laws governing special education. This the author knows through experiences of authorizing those payments under P.L. 94-142. A particularly alarming cost was $60,000 per year for children placed in private autism programs.

Our district's innovation was to create a regional site for public schools to send their children to at one of our public elementary schools. The district *made money* by saving the cost of private placement on this operation, and those children thrived. Districts can and do innovate, *and they can save money for the public by innovating*. That saved money, by law, goes back to the enterprise from which it came, public education. It is not taken as a profit.

Landing a financial grant did not earn the author a bonus or grant writer payment.[1] That financial fact did not stop the author from innovating. If you have to be profiting to motivate yourself to benefit children, then you are in the wrong business.

Long-standing private schools have endowments available for "deserving" applicants. It is telling that the financial failure rate of private schools is 67.8 percent, and that 41 percent of all private schools that were started in the 1990s no longer exist. This figure comes from Milwaukee, Wisconsin, a state that has had vouchers in place since 1991. Using public money to prop up schools that were not being chosen in a competitive *market is subsidizing a free-market competitor's losses with public funds. This is not a "free-market" solution.*

Most importantly, social capital and the value of all types of students learning together is lost when we school alone.

Our obligation as citizens to provide a free and appropriate education to our children is not an obligation to provide a consumer choice. We give up the social, political, and economic value of public education in these transactions with private contractors. When children from the same communities attend the same schools, there is a tremendous amount of social capital gained from those shared experiences. The first part of John Dewey's[2] quote regarding education in a democracy begins with parents who want the best education for their child:

What the best and wisest parent wants for his child, that must we want for all the children of the community. Any other ideal for our schools is narrow and unlovely, acted upon it destroys our democracy.

Intuitively we know this is true. Children learn from one another. Parents who are enlightened enough to want the best for their child, but also want that ideal for their fellow citizens, understand that they have a role as a community member to ensure all children are given an equal opportunity to thrive. There is truth in the oft-cited African adage that it takes a village to raise a child.

If a child hears a limited vocabulary in their home, they come to school without the background information they need to perform well academically. This is especially true of immigrant children, like the author's Italian parents during the 1920s. Social experiences[3] with other children can ameliorate this background information problem (Marzano, 2004; Marzano, 2007). When we remove the "high-performing" children from a group of children, all of those children lose out, including the high performers. This was the case when we segregated schools, and in the "good old days," when handicapped children were denied a free and appropriate public education.

If the best and wisest parents opt out of their public schools, they are also choosing to educate their children away from their fellow citizens. This individual choice based on a perceived consumer self-interest denies both the academically high-, middle-, and low-performing children the chance to learn together, a right they, as parents, have. What isn't a right is to expect their fellow citizens to finance this "consumer choice."

Incentivizing and removing these parents from the community's common school effectively removes a critical mass of the "best and wisest parents" from our publicly owned schools. These are the very people who will push a district to do better academically for every child. Public schools get better when all types of parents participate in the educational process, not because of charter or private school competition.

Charter schools labeling themselves "traditional" schools or "back to basics" implicitly acknowledge that public schools got it right in the "good old days."

We can do better than blindly following an economic theory that leads us to schooling alone in socially isolated schools. We do have a choice to make.

Do we want schools that are totally about our community's education or contracted businesses playing at being public schools (Fried, 2005)?

In the era of school "choice," parents can do something about the financial, political, and social issues raised by schooling alone and the privatization of public education. *They can choose.*

All citizens can choose to vote out representatives who have sold out our locally controlled public school facilities and ideals to private contractors.

Parents can also vote with their feet. In a word, "choice."

We can also choose charter providers that run their charters as a vital part of their communities' educational choices in a democratic republic in partnership with our publicly governed public schools. Dr. Budde's model for charter schools got that governance piece right.

We can choose to heed President Kennedy's call to service: "Ask not what your country can do for you—ask what you can do for your country," or we can choose to believe that "the only social responsibility of a business is to make a profit."

Which leader's words and ideas resonate with the American spirit?

We do have a choice. We need to choose wisely.

NOTES

1. These types of payments are common at privately held charter businesses. More than one charter management group was noted as paying itself $250 for each child passing the state tests. Isn't that supposed to be the primary product? Academic results.

2. Those reading Dewey's words so often in this book who believe he was promoting a "socialist" idea are advised to reflect on the fact that the Pledge of Allegiance was written by an avowed socialist clergyman, Francis Bellamy, in the 1890s. Liberty and justice for all is not a purely socialist or conservative ideal. It is an ideal of a democratic republic. So is a free and appropriate public education.

3. Critics of Dewey rightly cite his overemphasis of a social context for education at the expense of a common literacy for American school children. However, his ideals regarding ensuring our children learn together in common schools still ring true today. Anything less is unlovely and a threat to our democracy.

Bibliography

Bennis, W. G., Parikh, J., & Lessem, R. (1994). *Beyond leadership: balancing economics, ethics, and ecology*. Cambridge, MA: Blackwell Business.

Budde, R. (1988). *Education by charter: restructuring school districts: key to long-term continuing improvement in American education*. Andover, MA (290 S. Main St., Andover 01810): Regional Laboratory for Educational Improvement of the Northeast & Islands.

Dewey, J. (1891). *Outlines of a critical theory of ethics*. Ann Arbor, MI: Michigan Register publishing company.

Dyzenhaus, D., & Poole, T. (2015). *Law, liberty and state: Oakeshott, Hayek and Schmitt on the rule of law*. Cambridge, United Kingdom: Cambridge University Press.

Hirschman, A. O. (1970). *Exit, voice, and loyalty; responses to decline in firms, organizations, and states*. Cambridge, MA: Harvard University Press.

Knight, F. H., & Friedman, M. (1935). *The ethics of competition*. New York and London: Harper & Brothers.

Pojman, L. P., Vaughn, L., & Vaughn, L. (2014). *The moral life: an introductory reader in ethics and literature* (5th edition). New York: Oxford University Press.

Polanyi, M. (1952). *The Stability of Beliefs. British Journal for the Philosophy of Science*, 3(11), 217–32.

Polanyi, M. (1958). *Personal knowledge; towards a post-critical philosophy*. Chicago: University of Chicago Press.

Putnam, R. D. (2000). *Bowling alone: the collapse and revival of American community*. New York: Simon & Schuster.

Rawls, J. (1971). *A theory of justice*. Cambridge, MA: Belknap Press of Harvard University Press.

Schultz, E. (2011). *Retirement heist: how companies plunder and profit from the nest eggs of American workers*. New York: Portfolio/Penguin.

Society for Economic Anthropology (U.S.). Meeting (2006: Ventura, CA), Browne, K. E., & Milgram, B. L. (2009). *Economics and morality: Anthropological approaches*. Lanham, MD: AltaMira Press.

Virginia Polytechnic Institute and State University. College of Architecture and Urban Studies. (2000). The reflective practitioner. In (pp. v). Blacksburg, VA: College of Architecture and Urban Studies at Virginia Tech.

Vonnegut, K. (1997). *Timequake*. New York: G.P. Putnam's.

Wheatley, M. J. (2002). *Turning to one another: simple conversations to restore hope to the future* (1st edition). San Francisco, CA: Berrett-Koehler Publishers.

Index

501 C 3, 3, 113

academic performance, 3, 8, 59, 61, 92, 109, 117, 119, 121, 160
Adams, John, 32
American Federation of Teachers (AFT), 21
alternative schools, 59, 117
American Legislative Exchange Council (ALEC), 9, 96, 100
analogies, 101, 112, 113, 115
Anti-fragile, 166
Antioch New England, 42
Arizona: Arizona Christian School Tuition Organization, 14; Arizona State Board for Charter Schools, 69, 92, 101, 137, 169; AZ Christian Scholarship Fund, 54
authorization, 4

"backpacks full of cash," 10
Barnett, Lou, 100, 182
Bellamy, Francis, 14, 188
Brill, Steven, 111, 160
Brown v. Board of Education, 153, 179
Budde, Ray, 11, 16, 2, 15, 17, 34, 44, 46, 48, 75, 126, 188, 189
bureaucracy, 101
Byanylma, Winnie, 168

California, 10, 23, 135
capitalism, 6, 11, 15, 20, 111, 114, 116, 118, 165, 180, 183; capitalist, 11, 3, 15, 37, 55, 66, 96, 103, 115, 117, 111, 113, 168, 181
Capra, Frank, 117
Catch 22, 18
Catholic school education, 60
The Center for Media and Democracy, 100, 182
charter schools, 14, 17, 37, 109, 159, 165, 187
chief executive officer (CEO), 2, 3, 6, 13, 39, 50, 83, 87, 94, 112, 167, 168
Choate School, 181
Churchill, Winston, 50, 103
City Academy, 54
Civil War, 53, 86
Colorado, 23
Common Core, 8
common schools, 9, 13, 32, 34, 55, 78, 154, 157, 188
conservative, 3, 4, 55, 89, 100, 101, 108, 118, 121, 126, 129, 134, 138, 140, 145, 182, 188
consumer model, 3, 18
contracted services, 12, 121
corporate mindsets, 25
corporate welfare, 86

corporatization, 9, 10, 49
Credit Enhancements, 127

democracy, 9, 5, 32, 34, 42, 49, 53, 78, 86, 107, 108, 118, 111, 154, 158, 159, 168, 171, 175, 186, 187, 188
democratic republic, 10, 13, 15, 17, 20, 21, 31, 32, 34, 54, 55, 95, 107, 111, 113, 117, 150, 156, 159, 168, 175, 182, 185, 188
Dewey, John, 9, 5, 34, 78, 157, 186
Dichelle, Anne, 48
Dickens, Charles, 24
discriminate, 14
discrimination, 14
district, 10, 11, 16, 2, 3, 4, 5, 10, 11, 12, 13, 14, 15, 25, 26, 27, 28, 37, 38, 40, 44, 45, 46, 48, 49, 50, 51, 61, 67, 69, 73, 76, 80, 81, 83, 84, 89, 92, 94, 101, 103, 106, 107, 109, 114, 115, 118, 119, 124, 125, 126, 133, 134, 137, 138, 143, 146, 151, 153, 154, 159, 171, 175, 183, 186, 187
dropout rate, 65
Ducey, Doug, 63

The Economics of School Choice, 6, 105, 107, 109
educational model, 11, 16, 2
educational services, 10, 11, 16, 3, 4, 5, 12, 13, 27, 37, 40, 41, 42, 60, 75, 76, 79, 80, 81, 82, 84, 87, 101, 112, 113, 115, 117, 113, 115, 118, 121, 125, 139, 142, 171
Eisenhower, Dwight, 177
empowerment scholarship, 10
endowments, 186
entitlement, 7, 55, 79, 81, 114, 115, 180
entropy, 166
equalization formula, 38
Equalized Valuation Funding formulas, 37
equity, 67, 69, 118, 167, 172, 176
espoused theories, 171, 176, 185
Euclid, 32
exit theory, 3, 59, 60

factoring, 70, 93
false analogies, 109, 115
Fannie Mae and Freddie Mac, 10, 120, 128
Farnsworth, Eddie, 40, 167, 169, 170, 171, 172, 173
Federal Industry Regulatory Authority (FINRA), 128
The Federalist Papers, 88
financial meltdown, 57, 90, 95, 132
Fine, Michelle, 176
First Amendment rights, 185
forensic accounting, 18, 66
free market, 10, 11, 16, 3, 8, 10, 23, 24, 25, 27, 32, 39, 42, 50, 54, 55, 56, 57, 58, 59, 62, 65, 66, 67, 75, 76, 79, 83, 89, 95, 96, 98, 103, 108, 109, 112, 114, 115, 117, 118, 119, 120, 121, 124, 126, 132, 134, 140, 142, 143, 144, 151, 165, 166, 169, 171, 180, 181, 185, 186
free markets, 3, 58, 92, 95, 96, 108, 114, 117, 128, 132, 169
Friedman, Milton, 3, 13, 18, 20, 22, 24, 27, 35, 50, 51, 57, 58, 62, 79, 80, 103, 106, 109, 119, 113, 117, 118, 132, 139, 140, 154, 157, 160, 161, 162, 163, 165, 166, 167, 170, 172, 180, 181, 182, 183, 189

Gecko, Gordon, 103
General Accounting Office (GAO) standards, 163
general welfare, 78, 86, 87, 88, 101, 109, 113, 160
Glenn Way, 164
Goldwater, Barry, 57, 58
governance, 10, 11, 16, 2, 3, 7, 13, 17, 18, 29, 46, 48, 87, 94, 175, 183, 188
Grand Canyon Institute, 39, 59, 66, 67, 94, 103, 123, 137, 171
Greatest Generation, 6, 115, 159, 162
Gregg, Judd, 89
Gulan Schools, 80, 121

Index

Harris, Craig, 164
Hartford Current, 48
Hayek, Friedrich, 103, 180, 181, 189
Heller, Joseph, 17, 18
Hobson's choice, 32
Hot Shot team, 150
Hoxby, Carol, 105, 119
Hyde, Henry, 100, 182

Individuals with Disabilities Education Act, 43
intercepts, 97
It's a Wonderful Life, 117

Jefferson, Thomas, 32, 80, 183
Jensen, Michael, 167
junk bond, 10, 57, 86, 96, 109, 115, 120, 124, 126, 132, 135, 141, 147

Kennedy, John F., 160, 180
Kennedy, Ted, 89
Kentucky, 54
King Jr., Martin Luther, 57, 58
Koch, David, 103, 113, 182
Kroc, Ray, 165

leased employees, 72
Lewis, Sinclair, 24
Libertarian, 76, 78, 79, 80, 86, 87, 89, 90, 103, 111, 113, 114, 158, 179, 182, 183
Libertarians, 24
Lion's Club, 107, 111
long-term lease-adjusted debt, 67, 69, 124, 128
long-term leases, 93, 98

mainstreaming, 105
McAuliffe, Christa, 90, 169
McCarthyism, 118
McDonald's, 131, 165
McGuffey's Reader, 63
Meckling, William, 167
Meier, Deborah, 176
Meltdown, 6, 92, 94, 96, 98

Mencken, H. L., 86, 121
mercenaries, 117, 177
Minneapolis, 9
Minnesota State Legislature, 54
Monadnock Regional School Board, 51
Monopoly, 62
Morrill Act, 155, 156
Murphy District, 92

National Institute for Labor Relations Research, 24
National Labor Relations Act (NLRA), 24
National Right to Work Committee, 24
National Education Association (NEA), 21
Neighborhood Effect, 150
Net Gains, 65, 66, 67
net losses, 62, 92, 95, 138, 139
New Hampshire, 5, 12, 15, 28, 46, 48, 72, 89, 90, 106, 169, 176
New Market Tax Credit, 126
nonprofit, 13, 3, 98, 106, 128, 167, 172

Oklahoma, 23
oligarchies, 62, 101, 118, 160
overleveraged properties, 93
Oxfam International, 168

Pandora's box, 29
paradigm shift, 66
Performance Pay Initiative Proposition 301, 23
Pledge of Allegiance, 13, 14, 42, 188
private schools, 13, 11, 12, 38, 41, 42, 45, 62, 63, 65, 76, 96, 115, 118, 114, 121, 143, 166, 167, 170, 181, 186
property taxes, 37, 87, 114, 173
property-rich town, 37
Proposition 305, 23
Putnam, Robert: *Bowling Alone*, 18, 42, 78, 107, 116

Ravitch, Diane, 100, 117
Rawls, John, 42, 189

Reagan, Ronald, 4, 53, 89
Reign of Error, 101
related party transactions, 12, 40, 66, 113, 118, 138, 143, 159, 170
republic, 9, 13, 6, 15, 18, 20, 29, 31, 32, 34, 44, 54, 55, 76, 78, 88, 96, 100, 106, 107, 115, 117, 111, 113, 114, 149, 150, 157, 158, 159, 170, 179
research practitioner, 5, 66, 105, 106
Return on Investment, 65, 129
Rogers, Fred, 158
Roosevelt District, 92

Sanchez, Claudio, 54
Science, Technology, Engineering, and Mathematics (STEM), 156
Scrooge, 24
segregation, 41, 105
Senate Education Committee, 89
Sermon on the Mount, 5, 29
Side by Side Charter School, 48
social responsibility, 5, 13, 29, 58, 83, 103, 140, 165, 166, 188
socialist, 14, 62, 109, 188
Socrates, 106
Something Happened, 5, 15, 17, 18, 21
special education, 25, 26
state retirement system, 65, 66, 72, 83
subsidiary, 66, 72, 82, 83, 98, 106, 118, 124, 127, 128, 129, 130, 131, 169, 170
supreme court, 179

Teleb, Nicholas Nasisim, 166
The Theory of the Firm, 7, 167
theories in use, 72, 185

U.S. Department of Education (USDOE), 8, 14, 46, 73, 124, 140, 163, 164
U.S. Department of Labor Child Labor Laws, 21
under water, 9, 10, 57, 67, 69, 131, 132
University of Chicago, 16, 181, 189
University of Massachusetts, 16, 46
upside-down property, 93

Vonnegut, Kurt, 29, 108, 111, 161, 171, 190
voucher, 7, 15, 23, 40, 42, 45, 48, 54, 55, 56, 60, 66, 76, 79, 80, 96, 109, 112, 111, 114, 141, 154, 168, 182
vouchers, 9, 11, 13, 3, 8, 23, 29, 37, 45, 50, 61, 62, 76, 90, 108, 118, 121, 142, 154, 170, 181, 182, 186

Wall Street., 86, 103
West Virginia, 23

Yarnell Fire, 150

zero sum revenue game, 38

About the Author

Curtis J. Cardine has over 45 years of experience in education. Thirty of those years were in New Hampshire, where he founded the first public school charters while serving as superintendent of the Monadnock Regional School District. This endeavor was carried out with private funding and a 12.5 million DOE Grant. His business world background includes several small businesses including restaurants, gyms, and a start-up technology company. He currently is a research fellow for the centrist think tank, Grand Canyon Institute in Arizona.

Cardine's degrees are in elementary education with a mathematics minor, organization and management, and leadership and change. He was an active competitor in Olympic Weightlifting from 1969 through 2003; during that time he won gold, silver, and bronze medals at the international level including a silver at the World Cup in 1983.

The charter schools he founded in New Hampshire are still in business and were featured in *American Schools* by Sam Chatlin published by Rowman & Littlefield.

Cardine was a regional director of the Coalition of Essential Schools, a member of the Northeast Superintendent's Group, and a member of ASCD since its inception.

The core of his career was spent as a teacher in public schools. This experience includes teaching in K, 2, 4, 5, 6 grades, middle school and high school mathematics, gifted education, and computer sciences. He has served as an adjunct professor for undergraduate and graduate level courses at Franklin Pierce College, Keene State College, and Antioch New England.

Cardine led several schools as principal including a new start-up charter school in Arizona in 2010 (K–8). He has been a superintendent at the district level in New Hampshire and a superintendent of a charter group in Arizona.

His financial background is extensive in private business, school finance, and as a guest lecturer at the graduate level (Topic: Finding and Correcting Accounting and Financial Issues in Public Entities).

An abiding passion for public education in our republic has led to two books, *Carpetbagging America's Public Schools* and *Schooling Alone*.

www.ingramcontent.com/pod-product-compliance
Lightning Source LLC
Chambersburg PA
CBHW061828300426
44115CB00013B/2293